JAPANESE FINANCIAL MARKETS AND THE ROLE OF THE YEN

Pacific books of related interest

Coming to Terms: *The Politics of Australia's Trade with Japan 1945–57*
Alan Rix

International Economic Pluralism: *Economic Policy in East Asia and the Pacific*
Peter Drysdale

Japan's Financial Markets: *Conflict and Consensus in Policymaking*
James Horne

Japan's Foreign Exchange Policy: *1971–82*
Ryjotaro Komiya and Miyako Suda

Soviets and the Pacific Challenge
Edited by Peter Drysdale

JAPANESE FINANCIAL MARKETS AND THE ROLE OF THE YEN

Edited by

Colin McKenzie
Michael Stutchbury

ALLEN & UNWIN
in association with
The Australia–Japan Research Centre, Australian National University

First published in 1992
Allen & Unwin Pty Ltd
8 Napier Street, North Sydney, NSW 2059 Australia

National Library of Australia
Cataloguing-in-Publication entry:

Japanese financial markets and the role of the yen.

  Bibliography.
  Includes index.
  ISBN 1 86373 240 3.
  ISBN 1 86373 239 X (pbk.).

  1. Finance—Japan. I. McKenzie, C.R.   II. Stutchbury,
  Michael, 1957–

332.0952

Set in 10/11.5 Plantin by Graphicraft Typesetters Ltd, Hong Kong
Printed by Kin Keong Printing, Singapore.

Contents

Tables   7

Abbreviations   8

Glossary   9

Contributors   10

Preface   11

1   Overview: Japanese financial markets and the international role
of the yen   13
Colin McKenzie and Michael Stutchbury

PART I   THE DEREGULATION OF JAPANESE FINANCIAL MARKETS

2   Recent developments in Japan's financial markets   27
Colin McKenzie

3   Japanese financial markets and the implementation of monetary policy:
a retrospective view   45
Ryuichiro Tachi

4   Japanese corporate finance and behaviour: recent developments and the
impact of deregulation   55
Paul Sheard

PART II   JAPAN AND THE WORLD ECONOMY

5   The global role of Japanese finance   75
Yoichi Shinkai

6   The role of the yen in the Pacific and world economies   87
Makoto Fujii

7   Japan's growing role as an international financial centre   97
Yoshio Suzuki

Part III   Pacific financial markets

  8   The impact of Japan's financial deregulation on Singapore and
      Hong Kong   107
      Ong Nai Pew

  9   The role of the yen in the Pacific region: New Zealand as a
      case study   119
      Peter Nicholl and Peter Brady

 10   Japanese financial deregulation and international economic policy
      coordination: some small-country observations   133
      Christopher Higgins

Appendixes: 1   Major regulatory changes in the Japanese financial system,
                  1979–89   144
              2   Japan's offshore market   150

Notes   152

Bibliography   160

Index   168

Tables

2.1 Japanese financial instruments available to small-scale investors   32
4.1 Trends in overseas bond issues by Japanese firms, 1965–87   57
4.2 Fund procurement by Japanese firms through overseas bonds, 1977–88   58
4.3 Sources of funds for Japanese companies by type of security issued, 1975–87   59
4.4 Proportional share ownership of listed Japanese firms by type of shareholder, 1950–87   64
4.5 Analysis of corporate interlocking among Sumitomo Bank and its top thirty shareholders   68
5.1 Capital imports by Asian–Pacific countries   77
5.2 Japanese foreign assets and liabilities, 1986 and 1988   80
5.3 Japanese direct investment   81
5.4 Japanese financial transactions with non-residents   82
6.1 Currency distribution of external medium term bank loans   91
6.2 Foreign loans by Japanese banks   92
6.3 Euroyen loans by Japanese banks   92
6.4 Medium and long term yen-denominated foreign loans (including Euroyen)   93
6.5 International bond issues   94
6.6 Yen-denominated foreign bonds (samurai bonds) in the Tokyo market   94
6.7 Share of national currencies in total identified official foreign exchange reserves   96
9.1 Reserve Bank of New Zealand foreign currency assets   122
9.2 New Zealand's overseas exchange transactions—analysis by currency   125
9.3 New Zealand's overseas debt, June 1987   126
9.4 International use of the yen   129
A2.1 Assets outstanding in the Japanese offshore market   151

Abbreviations

ASEAN	Association of South-East Asian Nations
DTC	Deposit Taking Companies
FY	Fiscal Year (April to March in Japan)
GNP	Gross National Product
MOF	Ministry of Finance (Japan)
MITI	Ministry of International Trade and Industry (Japan)
OECD	Organisation for Economic Cooperation and Development
OPEC	Organisation of Petroleum Exporting Countries
PACU	Pacific–Asian Currency Union
SIMEX	Singapore International Monetary Exchange
TB	Treasury Bill
TSE	Tokyo Stock Exchange

Glossary

Bankers' Acceptance   A bank-guaranteed short term trade bill

Call Market   A short term money market where the transactions are loans with maturities between half a day and three weeks and the participants are restricted to financial institutions

Chūki Kokusai Fund   An open-ended public and corporate bond investment trust that invests 50 per cent or more of the principal in medium term government bonds (chūki kokusai). The minimum denomination is ¥100,000 and withdrawal is at a day's notice

Commercial Paper   An unsecured promissory note issued by corporate entities (other than financial institutions) for the purpose of raising short term funds

Gensaki Market   This is a market for long term government securities, corporate bonds and other securities with repurchase agreements where the typical length of the repurchase agreement is three months

Money Market Certificate   This is a type of time deposit issued by banks whose interest rate is tied to the interest rate on certificates of deposit. In 1989, it had a maximum maturity of 24 months and a minimum denomination of ¥10 million

Samurai Bond   A publicly offered yen-denominated bond issued in Japan by a foreign borrower

Shibosai Bond   A privately placed yen-denominated bond issued in Japan by a foreign borrower

Shogun Bond   A publicly offered bond denominated in a foreign currency issued in Japan by a foreign borrower

Tokkin Trust Fund   A trust fund where the investor has discretionary control over the investment of the funds

Treasury Bill   A short term government bond (usually three or six months in maturity)

Zaiteku (or Zai-tech)   Literally financial engineering, but its broad meaning is sophisticated financial management

Contributors

Colin McKenzie Osaka University, Japan
Michael Stutchbury *Australian Financial Review*, Australia
Peter Brady Reserve Bank of New Zealand, New Zealand
Makoto Fujii Ministry of Finance, Japan
Christopher Higgins Commonwealth Department of the Treasury, Australia
Peter Nicholl Reserve Bank of New Zealand, New Zealand
Nai Pew Ong Monetary Authority of Singapore, Singapore
Paul Sheard Australian National University, Australia
Yoichi Shinkai Osaka University, Japan
Yoshio Suzuki Nomura Research Institute, Japan
Ryuichiro Tachi Ministry of Finance, Japan

Preface

This volume presents some of the papers written for a conference on 'The Impact of Developments in Japan's Financial Markets in Asia and the Pacific', held in Canberra and Sydney, Australia, from 2 to 4 November 1987.* The purpose of the conference was to enhance the understanding of the theoretical and empirical issues affecting recent Japanese financial deregulation and its impact on the rest of the world.

The volume first identifies some of the major regulatory and non-regulatory developments that have occurred in Japanese financial markets recently, and the impact these developments have had on the implementation of Japanese monetary policy and the microstructure of Japanese financial markets. The role of the yen in the international monetary system and the factors promoting and inhibiting the development of the yen's international role are then examined. Finally, the questions of how small countries can respond to international coordination and financial deregulation in Japan and the causes of and possible solutions to the apparent current account imbalances between the United States, West Germany and Japan are investigated.

The opinions expressed in this book are the personal views of the authors and do not necessarily reflect the views of any organisation with which they are associated.

The conference was jointly sponsored by the Australia–Japan Research Centre, Australian National University; the Foundation for Advanced Information and Research, Japan; and the Institute for Fiscal and Monetary Policy, Ministry of Finance, Japan. The organising committee comprised Peter Drysdale (chairman), Jeff Carmichael, John Cosgrove, Peter Jonson, John McBride, Colin McKenzie, Tom Nguyen, Paul Sheard and Deane Terrell, with helpful advice from Yuichiro Nagatomi and Taroichi Yoshida. We are grateful for financial support from the following organisations: the Foundation for Advanced Information and Research, the Australia–Japan Research

---

* Some of the other papers presented at the conference have been published elsewhere: Argy (1989), and Onitsuka (1989).

Centre, the Westpac Banking Corporation, AMP, and the National Australia Bank.

For the convenience of readers, chapter 1 gives an overview of the conference, which includes a summary of the papers and the discussions that followed them.

We acknowledge with gratitude the contributions of various people to the preparation of the final version of the manuscript. Ian Collins prepared a summary of the discussion at the Canberra session. Janet Healey edited the complete manuscript for accuracy and consistency of style. Maxine Fulton, Kim-Lan Ngo and Minni Reis wordprocessed the manuscript from original transcripts in various states of imperfection.

Colin McKenzie and Michael Stutchbury
October 1991

1 Overview: Japanese financial markets and the international role of the yen

Colin McKenzie and Michael Stutchbury

Over the past ten years major structural changes have occurred in Japan's financial markets. Japan has become both the world's largest creditor and its largest exporter of capital. In 1988 Japan's net external assets were $292 billion, and its exports of capital in the same year were around $80 billion.* In contrast, the United States changed from being the world's largest creditor nation in 1982 (with the possible exception of Saudi Arabia on some estimates) to its largest debtor country in 1986, mainly because of its trade and budget deficits. As a result of continuing current account deficits since 1986, which have made it the world's largest importer of capital, the net overseas debt position of the United States has continued to worsen.

At the same time, Japan as a whole, and Japanese financial institutions (particularly life insurance companies), have become important players in the United States' financial markets and holders of significant amounts of bonds issued to finance the United States budget deficit, and Japanese companies have engaged in overseas takeovers quite actively. All these changes indicate shifts in the balance of global economic power. Some commentators have even hazarded that these changes are rooted in a deeper systemic weakness in the international financial system, and that the instability of financial markets (best illustrated by the crash of October 1987), exchange rate instabilities and the persistence of trade deficits are symptoms of that weakness. At the very least the 1987 crash highlighted the speed with which information flows among international financial markets, and the close connection between those markets. Japan's emergence from that crash in relatively good shape focuses attention on the characteristics of Japanese financial markets and institutions. As a result of these changes and trends, much attention has been concentrated on Japanese financial markets; on the future role of the yen in

---

* Throughout this book, unless otherwise stated, the dollar sign refers to the US dollar.

the international monetary system; and on the effect of Japanese financial deregulation on the countries of the Pacific.

This book raises a number of pertinent questions. How far has financial deregulation progressed in Japan, and what has been its domestic impact? What developments are likely to promote the role of the yen in the international monetary system, and what costs and benefits will that bring? What has been the impact of Japanese financial deregulation, both internationally and in the Asian and Pacific nations in particular?

This chapter attempts to identify the themes and summarise the arguments in the body of the book, as well as to provide some critical commentary, based in part on comments from discussants at the conference where the papers were originally presented. The remainder of the book falls into three parts: the deregulation of Japanese financial markets; Japan and the world economy; and Pacific financial markets. Chapters 2, 3 and 4 (part I) discuss the details of deregulation in Japan's financial markets (McKenzie); and the domestic macroeconomic and microeconomic impacts of these changes (Tachi and Sheard). Chapters 5, 6 and 7 (part II) focus on Japan's international role in the world economy (Shinkai); the international role of the yen (Fujii); and Japan's role as an international financial centre (Suzuki). Chapters 8, 9 and 10 (part III) are case studies of the effects of financial changes in Japanese markets on Singapore and Hong Kong (Ong); New Zealand (Nicholl and Brady); and Australia (Higgins).

The deregulation of Japanese financial markets

The three chapters of part I deal with Japanese financial deregulation and its domestic impact. McKenzie in chapter 2 summarises the recent regulatory changes that have occurred in Japanese financial markets. In chapter 3, Tachi examines the impact of these changes on the implementation of monetary policy in Japan, while Sheard in chapter 4 discusses their impact on the main-bank system and the microstructure of Japanese financial markets.

McKenzie provides an overview of the regulatory changes that have occurred in the Japanese financial system over the past ten years and background information for a number of the other chapters. He focuses on how deregulation has changed three areas that were viewed as features of the traditional financial system in Japan: interest rate determination; the segmentation of business activities; and the regulation of international capital flows.

On the question of interest rate deregulation, he notes that most interest rates are now market determined or set in relation to market interest rates. For example, rates on deposits over ¥10 million with the banking system are now market determined, while those over ¥1 million can earn market related interest rates. This is quite a change from the earlier interest rate regime (and the regime that still applies to interest rates on bank deposits of less than ¥1 million), where changes in deposit rates (and lending rates) were linked to changes in the official discount rate.[1] This should go a long way towards eliminating whatever 'unfair' cost-of-capital advantage Japanese corporations had as a result of the regulated system.

Another point discussed by McKenzie is that the segmentation of the business activities of financial institutions is reflected in the types of assets they can offer. The distinction between banks and securities companies has narrowed; securities companies may now take deposits through chūki kokusai funds, but they are still not able to make loans.[2] On the other hand, banks are still restricted domestically in their ability to deal in and underwrite securities. It is important to realise that banks are permitted to hold and trade corporate shares, a point of great importance to the main-bank relationships discussed in chapter 4 by Sheard. The importance of the differences in the permitted activities of financial institutions in different countries is also broadly addressed in chapter 7 by Suzuki.

Most formal restrictions on capital inflows and outflows have now been abolished but this can pose problems when different regulations are in place in the domestic and offshore markets, as indicated in the later discussion of chapter 6 and in chapter 7. The evidence cited by McKenzie suggests that the lack of capital controls means that covered returns in Japan and overseas have been equalised; but the same cannot be said for expected returns (incorporating expected exchange rate changes) on assets denominated in different currencies. The importance of the foreign exchange law of 1980 in allowing Japanese net savings to flow overseas is a recurrent theme in this and other chapters.

In chapter 3 Tachi provides details of some of the structural factors that led to the deregulation discussed in chapter 2; for instance, changes in the flow of funds, changes in the foreign exchange law in 1980, changes in interest preferences, and changes in the issues of government bonds. The chapter centres on how the implementation of monetary policy has changed, and Tachi depicts the evolution from a bank-credit-control paradigm of the 1950s and 1960s towards an open-market paradigm.

Japanese monetary policy in the 1950s to the 1970s relied on changes in the call rate and window guidance to influence bank lending behaviour and thus influence firms' investment decisions. While the existence of credit rationing in the loan market has been widely accepted, Tachi points out that the reason for this credit rationing, whether due to asymmetries of information, slow adjustment of the loan interest rate to its equilibrium level or the setting of the loan interest rate below its equilibrium level, must be the subject of more debate, and is important for the implementation of monetary policy. It seems that until 1975 slow adjustment of the loan interest rate was important, but after 1975 informational asymmetries became important. The speed of adjustment of loan interest rates to changes in officially set interest rates seems to have quickened as a result of deregulation.

Changes in corporate financing—together with securitisation and the increased borrowing opportunities at home and abroad provided as a result of deregulation—have also made it increasingly difficult for the Bank of Japan to influence economic activity by influencing interbank rates. Hence the need has arisen for the Bank of Japan to use open money markets, including a treasury bill market, with a clientele extending beyond financial institutions, in order to implement monetary policy to affect medium and long term interest rates. The need for a well developed treasury bill market is also raised in chapters 6 and 9 as a means of increasing the attractiveness of the yen as a currency for central banks to invest.

As for the implementation of monetary policy, Tachi suggests that the low substitutability between money and other assets, the stability of the money demand function, and the perception that policy was credible are reasons for Japan's success in controlling money supply and prices.

As pointed out in chapter 2, there are few explicit restrictions on capital inflows into Japan. Despite this, there have been few attempted (unfriendly) takeovers of Japanese firms by foreign firms (or by Japanese firms). One important reason for this is the existence of interlocking shareholdings which act to prevent external takeovers. These interlocking shareholdings are a crucial element in the 'main-bank system'.

The main-bank system, in which most large Japanese firms have a close relationship with at least one major bank, a relationship that incorporates lending, shareholding and informational elements, is one feature of Japanese financial markets that differentiates them from their United States counterparts. Sheard argues that the main banks perform three roles—risk bearing, monitoring and corporate control—which in American-style markets are typically performed by market institutions. He also suggests that the main-bank system is closely connected with the lifetime employment system and the lack of a well developed market for managers.

As Sheard points out, the impact of financial deregulation on corporate finance and the main-bank system is related to the reasons for the existence of the main-bank system: the main-bank system may be nothing but a product of regulation and the economic rents accruing to certain financial institutions as a result of regulation (or may have an internal economic logic that is dependent on regulation). Alternatively, the internal economic logic of the system may be largely independent of regulation. Sheard does not come down strongly on either side of the argument about the effect of deregulation on the main-bank system, the involvement of main banks in interlocking stockholdings and consequently the takeover market. However, he does suggest that the stance of the regulatory authorities, particularly the Ministry of Finance, towards takeovers of Japanese firms in general, and takeovers by foreign firms in particular, will be one important area to watch, even though there are few explicit restrictions on capital inflows today.[3]

Sheard's paper elicited conflicting reactions from conference members.[4] Rapp suggested that, while overseas securities issued by Japanese companies had increased, it was in fact Japanese financial institutions that were purchasing the securities; and he speculated that the funds were really being raised from Japanese banks rather than 'offshore'. As a result, he argued, there was an even tighter relationship between banks and companies than had been suggested by Sheard.

On the other hand, Miller argued that the important function of the main-bank system was risk bearing. He suggested that a complete breakdown of the main-bank system was the most likely outcome of financial deregulation, because companies are engaging in greater risk taking, not only in financial management but as they approach the cutting edge of technology. Takahashi commented that the main banks are here to stay, and will increase the scope of their operations to meet the changing needs of their clients by providing asset and liability management services and merger and acquisition facilities.

Japan and the world economy

Part II deals with some of the international issues that Japan must consider given its increasing international importance. These range from issues relating to Japan's role as a supplier of capital and the international impact of Japanese macroeconomic policy (discussed by Shinkai in chapter 5) to the role of the yen in the international economy (examined by Fujii in chapter 6) to questions Japan must face if Tokyo is to become a world financial centre (explored by Suzuki in chapter 7).

In discussing Japan's role as a capital exporter, Shinkai points in chapter 5 to an important distinction between Japan's being a net exporter of capital and Japan's engaging in maturity transformation. The former requires Japan to be running a current account surplus, while the latter involves borrowing short and lending long. Japan has been doing both quite actively. The elimination of most controls on capital inflows and outflows, as discussed in chapter 2, has been important in this regard; for example, the net external short term asset position of the Japanese banking sector worsened from minus ¥2.1 trillion in 1985 to minus ¥11 trillion in 1986, the year that the Japan offshore market was established, even though the banking system's net position in that market was close to zero (Bank of Japan 1988b: 19).

The macroeconomic policy stance in both the United States and Japan will be among the factors affecting both Japan's current account position and the net amount of capital that Japan exports.[5] In the context of discussion about Japan's use of fiscal and monetary policy to stimulate the world economy, it is important to realise that there is argument about the size and direction of the impact of Japan's monetary and fiscal policy on its current account position (and the current account positions of other countries), but that the impact seems to be small. In the conference discussion of this point, McKibbin agreed that Japanese fiscal policy has little effect on the United States trade balance, but suggested that the same could not be said for the trade balance of countries like Australia.[6] A number of countries have been pushing for a lower Japanese current account, and this effectively amounts to discouraging

Japanese capital exports. Lower Japanese capital exports, which will lower Japan's net contribution to world savings, can be expected to push up world interest rates, and could be particularly important for small countries like Australia importing capital from Japan (see also chapter 10). At the same time, some American interests have been pushing to maintain the active participation of Japanese investors in the United States bond markets.[7]

Shinkai makes another important distinction—that between asset accumulation and portfolio allocation. While the current account is the cap on Japan's net asset accumulation with the rest of the world in any year, within that limit there are choices to be made about the types of assets to be held, their currency denomination, and their maturity. In Japan, investment has concentrated on foreign-currency-denominated securities of the advanced countries, followed by direct investment and long term loans. Another conference paper also discussed this issue (Takagaki 1987). Since capital controls have been largely deregulated on these items, they will not increase appreciably as a result of recent deregulation. Shinkai suggests that the important factors influencing these investments are liquidity risk, default risk and exchange risk.

Internationalisation of the yen refers to the extent to which the yen is used as an invoicing currency, as a financing currency, and as an intervention currency. Of course, deregulation and internationalisation are not unconnected, since open and diversified markets in yen assets seem to be required before some central banks and individuals will hold yen assets, and since the extent to which the yen can be used as a financing currency depends on restrictions in the Euroyen market and in domestic financial markets. Fujii in chapter 6 provides a wealth of data about the yen's use in these three ways, and implicitly stresses the role the Japanese government can play in determining whether the yen will be internationalised.

Two arguments concerning what will determine whether the yen will become internationalised were raised at the conference. One highlights the role of the Japanese government in changing regulations in the financial system and in implementing monetary and fiscal policy. The other stresses the role of the market, since it is private sector agents who determine the currency in which they denominate their trade and financing contracts. Fujii implicitly supports the former argument, but this was strongly contested by Yoshitomi, whose comments support the latter argument (see also Yoshitomi 1987). A careful examination of the three uses of the yen would suggest, however, that both arguments have some validity, and chapter 9 suggests that the factors motivating foreign central banks' holdings of foreign exchange reserves are also important.

Even for Japan, only a third of exports and a little over 10 per cent of imports are denominated in yen. Financial deregulation has probably eliminated the non-availability of trade financing in yen as a reason for not denominating contracts in yen. The traditional view of the currency denomination of trade contracts suggests, first that internationally traded primary commodities are traded in dollars because the organised spot markets for these commodities determine dollar prices; and second, that there is a tendency for pricing in the exporter's currency to predominate in bilateral trade among countries with convertible currencies, particularly for heterogeneous commodities where the exporter has a degree of monopoly power (see McKinnon 1979: ch.4; Magee and Rao 1980).

The first hypothesis suggests that a shift in Japanese imports away from those primary products is likely to increase the proportion of import contracts denominated in yen. At face value the second hypothesis seems incorrect, since if both parties have identical expectations about future exchange rates the exporter will be indifferent about the currency denomination. Recent papers suggest that the currency denomination issue is an important mechanism in determining the timing of contract deliveries, but that the currency denomination depends on firm-specific characteristics—the weight an importer gives to the timeliness of delivery; differences in expectations about the exchange rate; the risk averseness of traders; and whether the international transactions are intra-firm or not—as well as on country-specific characteristics like the extent of uncertainty about inflation (see, for example, Mirus and Yeung 1987; Reagan and Stulz 1989). The argument suggests that Japan's low and fairly predictable inflation rate should work to increase the share of exports denominated in yen.

The yen's share in the world's foreign reserves is only 7 per cent. One reason for this is that central banks usually intervene in the foreign exchange market by buying and selling dollars against their own currencies, a point also stressed in chapter 9. Whether the yen assets currently available in Japan are enough to meet a particular central bank's requirements or whether a treasury bill market needs to be developed for this purpose depends on the emphasis that the central bank puts on liquidity and security.

Again this point elicited conflicting reactions from conference members. Suzuki questioned the need for a treasury bill market to service central bank desires for yen reserves, pointing to yen-denominated government bonds and bank deposits as ways to hold foreign exchange reserves as well as other very safe and liquid instruments in Tokyo, like certificates of deposit and gensaki agreements. Sirivedhin indicated that the central bank in Thailand had experienced no liquidity difficulties in the use of the yen in its foreign exchange reserves, as it had used the Bank of Japan's securities facilities. On the other hand, Sabirin suggested that the yen was not attractive to the central bank in Indonesia because of the lack of short term markets, and that this interacted with the process of decisionmaking in the central bank that focused on liquidity, security and yields. A similar point is made in chapter 9 by Nicholl and Brady.

It is as a financing currency that the yen has probably made its greatest gains in recent times, coinciding with the liberalisation of capital controls. There is one important caveat to this observation: in some areas, controls on domestic financial markets are stronger than those in the Euroyen market, and this has —not surprisingly—caused Japanese borrowers to switch to Euroyen markets (a trend also perceptible in Sheard's data), apparently increasing the yen's international role and the international function of Japanese banks. Further domestic deregulation is likely to bring some of these activities back to Japan.

Fujii suggests that the desirability of the internationalisation of the yen can be viewed from a world perspective, where it will help to diversify risk and increase the stability of the world monetary system (a point Suzuki stresses in chapter 7); or from the perspective of Japan, where there are concerns that it will undermine domestic monetary policy and increase exchange rate instability. Since private sector agents are already free to buy and sell yen-denominated assets (which may lead to exchange rate movements), it is difficult to see why the development of a treasury bill market will lead to any further exchange rate instability. The direct benefits to Japan in promoting the international use of the yen were strongly questioned by Yoshitomi in his comments on the paper; however, if all that prevents some central banks from holding yen assets is the lack of a treasury bill market, the development of such a market should at least lead to lower government financing costs.

Suzuki argues in chapter 7 that a stable financial system is one of the most important policy problems. Stability in this regard has two important aspects: the first is a consistent financial system in both the Japanese economy and the international financial system, with a lack of consistency likely to lead to further deregulation. Suzuki notes that differences in regulation and competition between systems are becoming more important. One could add to this differences in taxation, as alluded to in chapters 8 and 10. While facilities for lenders of last resort and deposit insurance in Japan do not differ from those in other industrial countries, Japanese practices of collateralisation, entry and exit in banking, bank supervision and separation of business areas do differ (see chapter 2). Sheard's discussion in chapter 4 suggests that the takeover market could be added to this list. Second, stability also covers the ability of the financial system to perform its established tasks of intermediation, risk avoidance and facilitating payments. Suzuki suggests that increased systemic risks (interest rate risk, liquidity risk, exchange rate risk) have increased with financial deregulation, and he highlights the need for policies to avoid systemic risk where possible.

Suzuki notes that Japan's international role is not limited to promoting the use of the yen as an international currency (although there may be little it can actually do, as discussed earlier), but will extend to becoming a supplier of public goods. On the supply of finance, Suzuki sees Japan's markets, both domestic and offshore, as recycling institutions, providing a complement to overseas markets and a centre for gathering information.

Pacific financial markets

Most discussion of Japan's financial role is from the perspective of either Japan or the United States; material about Japan's role from the perspectives of Asian–Pacific nations is sadly lacking. The papers in part III should help to redress that omission, since they discuss the impact of changes in Japanese financial markets on Australia, Hong Kong, New Zealand and Singapore.

Each of the three chapters has a different focus. Ong in chapter 8 examines the impacts on particular financial markets in Singapore and Hong Kong; in chapter 9 Nicholl and Brady investigate the use of the yen in New Zealand's trade and financing transactions; and Higgins in chapter 10 analyses the broad impact of Japanese financial deregulation on Australia and Australia's policy responses.

Ong examines the extent to which developments in Tokyo's financial markets have influenced Hong Kong and Singapore in five areas: international banking; foreign exchange transactions; bond markets; fund management; and futures markets. He suggests that the important determinants of the location of these financial activities are the sizes of the domestic and neighbouring markets; the concentration of players in the market; taxes and costs; and regulations. Ong hence provides a useful illustration of the importance of differences in regulation and an indication of some of the factors holding back the Tokyo market that were also discussed by Suzuki. Broadly speaking, he argues that Japan has the advantage in terms of the size of its domestic market, but not in terms of taxes, costs and regulations. The concentration of players depends on the specific market. One factor working strongly in favour of the Singapore and Hong Kong markets is that borrowers, particularly those on a small scale and with established reputations in these markets, are not likely to shift their borrowing to Japan suddenly if they do not have an established reputation there.

Bryant suggested in his commentary that the reference in the paper to the growth of the Tokyo market at the expense of other markets was overdone because in dealing with the introduction of new offshore markets we are not in a zero-sum world. Complementarities are likely to exist between markets, so that growth in Tokyo may lead to growth in other markets.

As with the internationalisation of the yen, there are two competing reasons for the internationalisation of finance. The first is the government policy hypothesis: that the government has lowered the separation fences around national financial markets, although there is still no single world financial market. The second is the non-policy hypothesis: that internationalisation occurs because of advances in technology and transportation or because financial institutions are following or leading corporate clients abroad. Ong focuses on the first and implicitly ignores the second. A contrary view was put forward by Bryant in the discussion when he suggested that generally it is the non-policy forces that are important, and propounded that the development of the offshore markets of Singapore and Hong Kong illustrates this, even though in Singapore there were some policy changes. In the case of Japan, however, he assumed that policy changes are important.

Nicholl and Brady provide a useful case study of the role of the yen in New Zealand that nicely complements the general discussion in chapter 6. They offer some useful insights into why the New Zealand central bank holds various currencies, and about the types of assets in its foreign currency reserves, together with a lot of information that is hard to obtain outside central banks.[8]

Nicholl and Brady suggest that the floating of the New Zealand dollar has itself provided the incentive to diversify reserve holdings, although the generality of this proposition needs to be qualified in the light of the Bank of New Zealand's stance of non-intervention, which is at odds with the practice of most central banks. A second important factor, they claim, is the need for low-risk instruments; thus, even while yen assets in the form of bank deposits with a market-determined interest rate can be obtained, there is a preference by the New Zealand central bank for government issued debt. They advance a number of reasons why the gensaki market in Japan does not meet that preference, and why a treasury bill market is required. This would seem to provide a decisive answer to the question raised earlier in the discussion of chapter 6; there are central banks whose holdings of yen assets are restrained by the lack of a treasury bill market. At the same time it explains why, despite extensive deregulation of financial markets in Japan, the yen's use as a reserve currency has not increased as much as Japanese officials and economists anticipated in the early 1980s. They underestimated the importance of government issued assets like treasury bills for foreign central banks.

The concentration of American dollars in New Zealand's trade, financial flows and turnover on the foreign exchange market is another reason why foreign exchange reserves remain largely in dollars. One interesting phenomenon noted by Brady and Nicholl is that the yen has been an important financing currency for the public sector, but not for the private sector in New Zealand. (Higgins in chapter 10 notes a similar trend in the past in Australia.) This, they suggest, is partly due to the preference in the private sector for borrowing short term rather than long term.

Brady and Nicholl are largely negative about the likelihood of a yen currency bloc (along the lines of the former sterling bloc), involving New Zealand and Japan, forming in the Pacific in the near future. In addition, the different trade structures and net overseas financial positions of Japan and New Zealand suggest that the real exchange rate adjustments required in the two countries after an economic shock will be different—a factor that works against any linking of the New Zealand dollar with the yen.

Higgins reinforces a point made in chapter 5 that one of the most important consequences of Japanese financial deregulation is the greater access of foreign borrowers to Japanese savings. Of course, this also means that marginal changes in Japanese capital flows are likely to have a major influence on the financial markets of small, open economies like Australia. Higgins points out that Australian macroeconomic policy has been influenced by both the size of and the changes in Japanese purchases of Australian securities. Some observers have gone even further than this, suggesting that the Reserve Bank has been targeting the exchange rate between the yen and the Australian dollar as a result of the increased financial flows between Australia and Japan.

On the microeconomic side, Australian state and federal governments and government instrumentalities have taken advantage of the new yen borrowing opportunities in bond markets opened up by Japanese deregulation, but private sector borrowers have not done so. But the private sector has borrowed significant amounts from Japanese banks and life insurance companies in the form of loans—borrowings that have been facilitated by recent financial deregulation in both Australia and Japan (see, for example, the data collected in McKenzie 1986).

Higgins makes another important point—that liberalisation and expansion in one market can generate pressures for change not only in other financial markets but in non-financial markets as well. The point is illustrated by both the Japanese and the Australian experience: for example, the impact on the wage fixing system of the floating of the Australian dollar in 1983 and its subsequent depreciation. Of course, the pressures can be generated in both home and foreign markets. A similar point was made in another conference paper (Rapp 1987), and by Rapp in his comments on McKenzie's paper.

Although a relatively small country like Australia is not represented in discussions of international economic coordination, it is affected by the policies implemented as a result of those discussions. Higgins suggests that such countries need to voice their interests to those countries that are represented at these discussions, or alternatively form coalitions to ensure that their voices are heard. By and large, though, countries like Australia must accept that they are price takers, and must try to ensure that their economies adjust to changes in the external economic environment.

Looking a little to the future, the following possible regulatory changes in Japanese financial markets are likely to have important international impacts: the deregulation of the domestic bond and debenture markets, which will probably bring back onshore a portion of such business currently conducted offshore; the development of a treasury bill market, if only because some central banks have strong preferences for liquid, government-issued securities; the deregulation of controls in product markets for life insurance companies, which constitute one of the main groups of Japanese investors overseas (see, for example, McKenzie 1988); and the relaxation of controls on the portfolio choice of the postal savings system, which could be especially important given that almost one fifth of the personal sector's financial assets are invested with that system. Given the way deregulation has occurred so far, these further changes can be expected to take place step by step.

PART I

The deregulation of Japanese
financial markets

Part I deals with the structural changes in Japan's financial system over the past ten years and how they have influenced the implementation of monetary policy in Japan and the microstructure of Japanese finance. In chapter 2 McKenzie summarises recent regulatory developments in the Japanese financial system, and this chapter contains background information that is drawn upon throughout the book. Chapter 3, by Tachi, discusses some of the structural factors leading to Japanese financial deregulation and how the implementation of monetary policy in Japan has changed since 1975. In chapter 4 Sheard examines Japan's main-bank system and how it might change as a result of financial deregulation, and offers important insights into whether an active takeover market will develop in Japan and whether foreign investors will be able to participate in that market.

2 Recent developments in Japan's financial markets

Colin McKenzie

In the early 1960s Japan's financial system was noted for the inflexibility of its interest rates, the compartmentalisation of its financial institutions, and its restrictions on capital flows. In the 1980s the system changed significantly in the extent to which its interest rates are market determined, and in the lessening of restrictions on capital flows between Japan and the rest of the world. However, there has been less change in the degree of market segmentation.

Financial reform is still proceeding in Japan. The main impetus for financial change arose initially because the country's financial markets could not absorb the massive issues of national government bonds resulting from the large budget deficits that began around 1975. The initial impact of these bond issues was on the market in long term assets. Although government deficits have been cut back to the extent that issuing deficit-financing bonds was expected to be unnecessary in the 1990 fiscal year, the refinancing of maturing debt is providing a new and continual stimulus to financial change. The introduction of new computing and telecommunications technology in the banking and finance sectors, and swings in the current account, have also played their part in promoting deregulation.

In the past, piecemeal rather than revolutionary change has been the rule for financial deregulation in Japan, and this pattern can be expected to continue. One reason for the pattern has been the administration's concern to minimise the potentially disruptive effects of deregulation—for example, the possibility of large flows of funds away from some markets or institutions. Another reason is that various institutions (and the Bureaus within the Ministry of Finance responsible for the particular institutions) have sought deregulation either to put themselves in more advantageous positions vis-à-vis other financial institutions, or to offset deregulation favouring another group of institutions (Horne 1985). This approach can lead to further deregulation.

Japan's revision of its foreign exchange law in 1980 opened up possibilities for the rest of the world to draw on Japan's savings and for Japan to become the world's largest exporter of capital. In 1985, net outflows of long term capital from Japan were \$64.5 billion, and by 1986 they had risen to \$131.5 billion; in 1988, they were still \$130.9 billion. At about the same time as Japan revised its exchange law, the United States, because of its budget deficits, became a significant drawer on world savings. It can be argued that the resulting rise of American interest rates was moderated to some extent by the availability of Japanese savings.

Rather than describing in detail the many regulatory changes that have occurred in Japan recently, this chapter indicates the broad trends of deregulation and identifies some of the issues that still remain unresolved. Details of the changes in rules and regulations are presented in appendix 1. The impact of financial deregulation on the implementation of monetary policy, in particular the change from a credit-control paradigm to open-market operations, is the focus of chapter 3.

The relaxation of interest rate controls is discussed in the next section. The principal remaining interest rate control is on small-denomination deposits, and the main barrier to relaxing this control is the postal savings system. The second section examines the relaxation of market segmentation, and notes that, while the business division between securities and banking has been relaxed somewhat, it remains broadly intact. In the third section, a brief review of the deregulation of Japanese capital flows is followed by a discussion of how Japan's financial integration with the rest of the world has been affected by financial deregulation. The interest elasticity of personal savings is the principal issue addressed in the fourth section.

In reviewing recent developments in Japan, this chapter will indicate where deregulation has or has not taken place and some of the potential problem areas.

Relaxation of interest rate controls

The relaxation of the strict controls on interest rates of the 1940s to 1960s has come about through two principal channels: the relaxation of interest rate controls on existing assets; and the introduction of new assets, with market determined rates or rates that are linked to market rates.

Examples of the former measure are the abolition of posted rates in the call and bill markets in 1979; and the lifting of interest rate controls on foreign-currency time deposits held by residents in 1980, and on large-denomination time deposits in October 1985. Examples of the introduction of new assets are the establishment of the certificate of deposit market in 1979; the bankers' acceptance market in 1985; the Tokyo offshore market in December 1986 (discussed by Ong in chapter 8); and a domestic commercial paper market in November 1987. Money market certificates, a form of time deposit with interest rates linked to the market rates of certificates of deposit, were also introduced in 1985.

Changes in the minimum denominations and permitted maturities for certificates of deposit, money market certificates and large-denomination deposits, and increases in the issue ratios for money market certificates and certificates of deposit, have substantially increased the availability of assets with deregulated interest rates (see appendix 1 for details). These changes illustrate the step-by-step approach to financial deregulation adopted by Japanese regulators: for example, the liberalisation of large-denomination deposits between October 1985 and October 1989 occurred in nine stages. Given the minimum denominations associated with each of these assets, these changes would have provided opportunities for firms wishing to invest on a fixed term basis rather than for individuals.

There have also been some changes in the method of determining yields on bonds issued by the government. It is only since February 1986 that short term government securities in the form of discount bonds of less than six months' maturity have been issued by public tender; and only since September 1989 have three-month treasury bills been issued. While Japan still lacks an active and deep market for short-term government securities, these developments can be interpreted as steps in that direction. The importance of an active and deep market for these short term government securities is that it should not only help to implement domestic monetary policy (see Tachi in chapter 2), but it should also eliminate a significant barrier to the development of the yen as a reserve currency (see Nicholl and Brady in chapter 9). This is because some governments and central banks have claimed that the lack of a well developed Japanese market in short term government securities has been an impediment to increasing their holdings of yen assets.

The further development of a treasury bill market is a well known source of conflict between the Bank of Japan and the Ministry of Finance. The Bank of Japan's support for the development of a treasury bill market arises from a desire to promote open-market operations as a tool of monetary policy. The Ministry of Finance, on the other hand, is concerned about the possible disintermediation effects on other markets, as well as about the impact of this new market on the cost of government borrowing.

A major stimulus for financial deregulation in Japan has been the massive issues of government bonds to finance the government's fiscal deficits since 1975. Initially, a bond underwriting syndicate composed of Japan's main financial institutions financed the debt. To increase the attractiveness of bonds, various measures have been adopted, including diversifying the maturities issued, shortening the time that syndicate members must hold bonds before they can sell them, and setting interest rates more flexibly. In setting the yields on underwritten bonds, the authorities have had to pay greater heed to market trends and the rates paid on other market determined instruments. These changes seem to have significantly narrowed the difference between the market yields in the secondary market for government bonds and the subscriber yields in the primary market (Pettway 1982). Although the syndicate is still the principal avenue for selling bonds, its relative importance has declined. The sale of certain government bonds by tender began in 1978, and now between 20 per cent and 30 per cent of issues are floated by competitive bidding.

For financial institutions, the liberalisation of interest rates has meant that, over time, an increasing proportion of their funds are bearing non-regulated interest rates. In the beginning of the 1983 fiscal year, for example, less than 15 per cent of the domestic funds raised by city banks paid market rates, whereas at the end of the 1988 fiscal year this proportion was estimated to have risen to nearly 55 per cent (Bank of Japan 1987: 46; 1989: 46). Similar but less pronounced trends can be observed for the fund raising activities of the regional banks and other banks. The Japanese corporate and personal sectors have also been shifting the use of their funds towards assets with non-regulated rates (Bank of Japan 1986b: 16; 1989: 45).

In June 1989 small-denomination money market certificates (termed super MMCs) with a minimum denomination of ¥3 million and a market related interest rate were introduced. Since the minimum denomination was reduced to ¥1 million in April 1990, small-denomination deposits (less than ¥1 million) have been the most important assets, with yields that are still below market rates. Money market certificates and large-denomination time deposits also provide deregulated interest rates for deposits greater than ¥10 million and with maturities of more than one month.

The importance of these minimum-denomination limits can be gauged by comparing them with savings levels. According to one recent survey (Chochiku Kōhō Chūō Iinkai 1989), average household savings in Japan in early 1989 were ¥10.13 million. The skew in the distribution of savings, with 32.8 per cent of those surveyed having savings of more than ¥10 million and 26.5 per cent having savings of less than ¥4 million, suggests that the average figure is a little misleading. On this evidence a significant proportion of Japanese households in 1989 could not use money market certificates, with their minimum denomination of ¥10 million, and a sizeable minority could not use super MMCs, with their minimum denomination of ¥3 million, even if they deposited all their savings in them. Hence, a further reduction in minimum denominations could bring significant benefits to a large proportion of Japanese households.

Interest rates on deposits at call and small-denomination time deposits at banks and post offices are still revised in the wake of changes in the official discount rate after consultations between the Ministry of Finance and the Ministry of Posts and Telecommunications. So, for example, the official discount rate was raised by half a percentage point in November and again in December 1989, and rates on time deposits rose by 0.37 per cent and 0.43 per cent respectively about a month after each rise. As the relative quantity of funds invested in instruments bearing market or market related interest rates increases, the importance of disagreements between the two ministries about the size of these rises will obviously decline.

However, problems with deregulating interest rates on small-denomination deposits centre on the role of the postal savings system. In September 1989, postal savings represented about 19 per cent of individuals' financial assets, or over ¥130 trillion. The sheer size of the postal savings system in the Japanese financial system has led some commentators to suggest that the system could become a price leader in a fully deregulated deposit market (Akiyama 1987).

Regulatory changes that favour the postal savings system have important implications for monetary authorities in defining and controlling the money supply. Intermediation and disintermediation between the banking system and the postal savings system have been important in the past for interpreting changes in the money supply, since bank deposits are included in the money supply, whereas those with the postal savings system are not. Policy changes that led to significant shifts in the allocation of funds across financial institutions—for example, the abolition in 1988 of the maruyū savings system that provided income tax exemption for interest earned on small-denomination deposits (discussed later in this chapter)—caused difficulties in interpreting money supply figures. This highlights a more fundamental issue: that deregulation poses a number of problems concerning the definition of the money supply, since the distinction between money and other assets is blurred.

There are two further arguments regarding interest rate deregulation and the postal savings system. First, the postal system does not face the same restrictions on its activities as other financial institutions, so that it engages in insurance, pension and banking business, as well as the sale of postal services. Thus it can take advantage of any economies of scope that exist among those types of businesses. Second, it is a government instrumentality, and so may set its deposit rates at non-commercial levels, given that it does not have to make a profit; or it may be able to cross-subsidise deposit rates from its profits from other business. In addition, the postal savings system is subject to the same payments risks as other institutions, but it is not clear who bears these risks.

One possible solution to this problem is to divide or privatise the postal savings system. An associated problem for the Ministry of Finance is that about 25 per cent of the funds for the government's investment program (the Fiscal Investment and Loan Program) come from postal savings (Bank of Japan 1986a: 388). The financing cost associated with this 25 per cent is likely to increase if interest rates on small-denomination deposits are liberalised, and this would add to the cost of financing the government's deficit. Offsetting this is the current efficiency cost of setting the wrong interest rates.

The focus on interest rates in the banking system and the postal savings system presents a slightly misleading impression of the investment opportunities available to small-scale investors. Table 2.1 provides an outline of some of the opportunities now open to such investors. As the table shows, there are assets with other financial institutions that offer market related interest rates on smaller deposits: for example, chūki kokusai funds with securities companies.

For loan rates there are still some rigidities in the setting of interest rates, with the long term and short term prime rates being set by the banks in consultation with the monetary authorities. The current rules are that the

Table 2.1 Japanese financial instruments available to small-scale investors

Financial institution	Financial instrument	Period	Pre-tax interest rate[a]	Interest rate type[b]	Minimum denomination	Cancellation provisions	Special features
Bank	Ordinary deposit	—	0.75%	—	¥1	At any time	Deposit/withdrawal at will
	Time deposit	6 mth	4.0%	F	¥100	Before 6 mths, interest rate is 0.75%, before 1 yr 3.25%	Can be combined with an ordinary deposit to form a Sōgō account that can be used for borrowing against the time deposit
		1 yr	4.75%	F			
	Super MMC[c]	6 mth	5.5%	F	¥3,000,000	Within 6 mths & 1 yr, interest on ordinary deposit and 50% of contracted interest rate respectively	Interest rate linked to average issue rate of certificates of deposit
		1 yr	5.5%	F			
		3 yr	5.5%	F			
Post office	Ordinary postal deposit	—	2.16%	—	¥10	At any time	Deposit/withdrawal at will
	Time deposit	6 mth	4.0%	F	¥1,000	Before 6 mths & 1 yr, interest rate is 0.75% and 3.25%	
		1 yr	4.75%	F			

Category	Name	Term	Rate	Type	Min. amount	Cancellation charge	Notes
Trust banks	Kinsen Trust	2 yr+ / 5 yr+	5.05% / 6.48%	V / V	¥5,000	Cancellation charge of 0.3% & 2.3% on 2 & 5 yr trusts	Dividend rate depends on bank's fund management. Cancellation possible at any time
	Hit	1 yr+	4.87%	V	¥100,000	Within a year, cancellation charge of 0.3% on principal	Cancellation at will after 1 yr
	Loan trust	2 yr / 5 yr	5.2% / 6.62%	V / V	¥10,000	Cancellation charge of 0.6% & 2.5% of principal on 2 & 5 yr trusts	Dividend rate depends on bank's fund management. Bank will repurchase after 1 yr
	Big	2 yr / 5 yr	5.2% / 6.62%	V / V	¥10,000	Cancellation charge of 0.5% & 3.1% of principal on 2 & 5 yr items	Freely convertible to cash after 1 yr
Bank debentures	Discount debentures	1 yr	5.607%	F	¥10,000	Can be sold at any time at market price. Securities tax of 0.03% payable	Return in the form of capital gain
	Interest-bearing debentures	3 yr / 5 yr	6.5% / 6.5%	F / F	¥10,000	As for discount debentures	

Table 2.1 (Cont'd)

Financial institution	Financial instrument	Period	Pre-tax interest rate[a]	Interest rate type[b]	Minimum denomination	Cancellation provisions	Special features
	High Jump	3 yr	6.5%	F	¥10,000	Charge of 2% & 1% for cancellations before and after 1 yr	
	Wide	5 yr	6.6%	F	¥10,000	Charge of 2%, 1% & 0.5% for cancellations within 3 yrs, between 3 and 4 yrs & after 4 years	
Securities firms	Chūki Kokusai Fund	—	4.854%	—	¥100,000	Cancellations within 30 days are subject to charge of 0.2% and tax of 0.03%	After 30 days, money can be withdrawn at one day's notice
	Bond investment trust	—	6.85%	V	¥10,000	At any time. Cancellation charge of 1.03% of principal	

		Term	Yield	F/V	Minimum	Liquidity	Notes
Government bonds	Long term bonds	10 yr	6.772%	F	¥50,000	At any time, bonds sold at prevailing price. Tax of 0.03%	Rate of return in the form of capital gain
	Discount bonds	5 yr	6.207%	F	¥50,000	As for long term bonds	
Insurance company	Single premium endowment insurance	3, 5, 10 yr	6.30% (5 yr)	V	¥0.1 – 1.0m[d]	At any time. Amount refunded depends on age of investor, maturity, etc.	Insurance premium paid up front
Others	Government bond term account	2, 3, 4, 10 yr	—	—	¥500,000	At any time, bonds sold at prevailing price. Tax of 0.03%	Interest on bonds invested in term deposit
	Government bond trust	2, 3, 4, 10 yr	—	—	¥300,000	As above	Interest on bonds invested in trust account
	Gold investment	1 mth 1 yr	6.25% 6.5%	F	300 grams 500 grams	In principle, not possible	3 & 6 mth accounts available

Notes: a Interest rates at 5 February 1990.
b F—fixed yield; V—variable yield.
c Post Office offers super MMCs (money market certificates) under the name of POST on identical conditions. The minimum denomination of this instrument will be reduced to ¥1 million from April 1990.
d Dependant on the company.

Source: *Money Japan*, April 1990.

short term prime rate is fixed at the Bank of Japan's discount rate plus 0.5 per cent, and the long term prime rate is fixed at the rate on bank debentures plus 0.9 per cent. However, as financial deregulation has led to the development of alternative domestic and overseas sources of funds (see Sheard in chapter 4), the importance of these prime rates has declined and greater heed of market developments has had to be taken in determining them. (Tachi in chapter 3 discusses in more detail how deregulation has affected the determination of interest rates in the loan market.) The city banks have recently been moving towards determining the short term prime rate using a weighted average of certain money market rates and regulated deposit rates.

Relaxation of market segmentation

Three areas of market segmentation in Japan have been noted: the distinction between long term and short term banking; the distinction between commercial and trust banking; and the distinction between banking and securities business.

There are two important types of banks in Japan: ordinary banks and long term credit banks. City banks are the most important of the ordinary banks. City banks obtain most of their funds from deposits. They are forbidden to issue debentures, and the term deposits that they can issue are limited to two years. Long term credit banks obtain funds mainly by issuing debentures. In fund raising, this distinction between long term and short term remains broadly intact, but if city banks were granted approval to issue Euroyen bonds, as resident foreign banks already have been, or were permitted to issue small-denomination money market certificates with maturities of more than two years, this could change substantially.

In the use of funds significant changes have occurred. From 1970 to 1985 the long term domestic lending of city banks increased from 25 per cent to 41 per cent of their funds. For long term credit banks the trend is otherwise: 88 per cent of their funds went to long term lending in 1970, but this had fallen to 73 per cent by 1985 (Fukuzawa 1987: 4). The maintenance of the distinction between long term and short term deposits on the liability side but not for lending on the asset side has created a mismatch in the maturity structures of both city banks and long term credit banks.

The broad division in Japan between commercial banking and trust banking that separates deposit collection and trust business has been maintained. Japan's population is ageing rapidly because of an increased life expectancy and a declining birthrate, and as a result pension trust business is a growth area and has attracted foreign interest; indeed, foreign banks have recently been admitted into trust business. However, proposals for domestic securities companies to join with foreign banks and engage in trust banking have not been approved, apparently because of a desire to maintain the distinction between trust banking and securities business. There are barriers against both domestic and foreign participants entering the trust business, and these entry barriers have been the subject of both domestic and foreign criticism.

The division between securities business and banking business arises from Article 65 of the Securities Exchange Law (which corresponds to, but does not precisely replicate, America's Glass–Steagall Act). The Article explicitly restricts banks from participating in securities business—for example, underwriting, and dealing in or distributing negotiable securities (except public bonds and public debentures). Until recently (even with respect to public bonds) administrative guidance permitted banks to underwrite only public bonds, which has created a distinction between banking and securities business. Unlike banks in the United States, Japanese banks have not been prevented from holding corporate shares; and banks are, in fact, significant shareholders in Japan, as discussed by Sheard in chapter 4.

The distinction between banking and securities business was narrowed when banks were permitted to sell government bonds and when they were allowed to deal in government bonds, first those with remaining maturities of less than two years (1984), and then all government bonds (1985). Somewhat later, foreign banks in Japan were permitted to deal in bonds and sell them directly to the public. For corporate non-public bonds, the distinction between banks and securities companies remains intact.

On the fund raising side, since 1980 securities companies have been able to market chūki kokusai funds, which are very like at-call deposits. Once money has been in the fund for one month, it is available at one day's notice, and in addition the fund has no minimum denomination, unlike bank time deposits. Money deposited in these funds is invested in medium term government bonds. The funds bear higher yields than one-year time deposits, and are also more liquid.

There is still strong pressure, especially from foreign banks in Japan, for further relaxation of Article 65 of the Securities Exchange Law. Japanese banks have been able to engage in securities business abroad in countries that do not distinguish between banking and securities business. However, foreign banks have not been able to establish subsidiary securities companies in Japan, although they have been permitted shareholdings of up to 50 per cent in a securities company. Even this is far more than domestic banks are able to do.

The removal of the barriers in these three areas could be beneficial by reducing the costs of financial intermediation through increased competition among institutions, and by permitting the exploitation of any economies of scope that exist between the various activities. On economic grounds it is difficult to justify the distinctions between long term and short term banking and between commercial and trust banking. Only with respect to the separation of banking and securities business can it be cogently argued that conflicts of interest and a reduction in 'sound banking' practices might arise if the separation were eliminated; and even then, the separation of the two types of business may not be the best way of meeting these objections. For example, the conflict of interest really refers to a principal–agent problem (the principal being the investor and the agent being the bank or securities company), where the incentives motivating the agent mean that the agent does not necessarily act in the principal's interest. Principal–agent theory suggests that it is the contract design that should be the focus of attention. In any case, in order to maintain the international competitive position of Japan's financial institutions, the Japanese authorities may be forced to remove the restrictions.

Deregulation of capital flows

After a brief review of the important remaining restrictions on capital flows, this section investigates the extent to which financial integration between Japan and the rest of the world has increased as a result of Japanese financial deregulation. Covered interest rate parity, uncovered interest rate parity and real interest rate parity are used as measures of financial integration (as suggested by Argy 1989), and empirical evidence is examined with respect to the integration of stock prices, the influence of international factors on Japanese bond prices, and currency substitution. The discussion also covers the impact of financial deregulation on capital flows and the exchange rate.

Remaining restrictions on capital flows

Until December 1980, capital flows between Japan and the rest of the world were in principle prohibited. There were, of course, exceptions, so it would be a mistake to conclude that little or no capital movement was allowed before then. However, since the new Foreign Exchange and Foreign Trade Control Law was implemented in December 1980, such flows have been in principle permitted. Before its implementation, considerable deregulation of international capital flows had taken place under the framework of the old law. The new law both ratified the changes up to that point and made possible more rapid deregulation in the 1980s. Two major explicit regulatory changes occurred at the same time: the removal of the ceiling on deposits in foreign currencies that residents could hold, and the deregulation of impact loans in foreign currencies (Komiya and Suda 1983). The right to require prior approval for capital transactions that are not specifically restricted is retained for emergencies.

Under pressure from the United States for Japan to liberalise its capital markets, a working group of officials from both countries was established to consider changes to the Japanese financial system. This group was known as the Working Group on the Yen–Dollar Exchange Rate, and a number of important changes occurred after the release in 1984 of its report on the yen–dollar exchange rate (Frankel 1984). These changes included the abolition of the 'real demand' principle for forward transactions, the abolition of regulations on the spot positions of foreign exchange banks, and the relaxation of various regulations on Euromarket transactions. Bank loans and securities transactions are virtually free from regulation. Foreign users and sources of funds are now substantial, which is certainly due to the deregulation of the 1980s.

A number of the important remaining foreign exchange restrictions under the foreign exchange law relate to Euroyen transactions, and these are designed to take account of the different degrees of regulation in the domestic and Euromarkets. While foreign exchange banks are free to accept both Euroyen deposits from non-residents and interbank Euroyen deposits, residents not engaged in banking are in principle prohibited from holding deposits in foreign countries. Since 1984, Euroyen certificates of deposit with maturities of up to six months can be issued freely by foreign exchange banks, but they must not be sold to residents. Euroyen loans to non-residents are free, but the banks have been asked to restrain their loans to foreign branches of Japanese businesses. For residents, short term Euroyen loans are free of restrictions, but medium and long term loans are subject to a similar voluntary restraint. There are restrictions concerning residents and non-residents who may issue Euroyen bonds, and, in the case of resident issues, on the sale of these bonds to residents. It is only since 1984 that resident firms have been authorised to issue Euroyen bonds. Differences in the pace and the extent of deregulation of domestic financial transactions and international financial transactions mean that in some areas the conditions applying to the Euroyen markets appear to be less restrictive than those in the domestic markets, which is leading to a significant expansion in the activities of Japanese banks overseas (Terrell *et al.* 1989).

There are still ceilings on investment overseas by private financial institutions (for example, life insurance companies and trust banks), although they do not appear to be binding at present. Until early 1986, investment by life insurance companies in foreign securities was restricted to 10 per cent of their total assets. By 1986, this had become a binding constraint for some of the larger life insurance companies. The limit was raised to 25 per cent in April 1986, and then to 30 per cent in August 1986. Concurrently with increases in the limits, some assets that had previously been outside the earlier limit were included—for example, foreign currency deposits with Japanese banks. Restrictions on the size of additions to these companies' stocks of foreign securities relative to the increases in their net funds were also relaxed, and then abolished in 1986.

Casualty insurance companies, annuity trusts and investment trusts are also subject to limits on their investment in foreign securities. However, these restrictions were substantially relaxed in July–August 1986. Restrictions on investment by foreign exchange banks in foreign securities were also lifted in October 1986. Relaxation of these restrictions (called 'private intervention' in Japan) appeared to be part of an attempt by the Japanese authorities to slow down the appreciation of the yen in 1986 by raising private demand for assets denominated in foreign currencies. Prohibitions on overseas investment by agricultural cooperatives and credit unions also began to be relaxed in 1986. Overseas borrowings and investments by some government instrumentalities are still subject to ceilings or prohibitions.

Issues by foreigners of yen denominated (samurai) and foreign currency denominated bonds (shogun) bonds are still restricted as to eligible issuers, the size of issues, and the maturity of issues. However, the eligibility criterion has been relaxed on a number of occasions recently.

The Tokyo offshore market opened in December 1986 as a centre for non-residents to raise and invest funds with preferential treatment with respect to reserves, interest rate controls and withholding taxes. The development of this market is important in enhancing Tokyo's role as a world financial market, and is fully discussed by Suzuki and Ong in chapters 7 and 8 respectively.

Financial integration

The mobility of capital across international borders can be measured by the degree to which covered interest rate parity holds and by the relationship between short-maturity prices and returns of shares listed on a number of stock exchanges. Several studies have found that covered interest parity between onshore yen and offshore dollar assets, while not holding for most of the 1970s, seems to have held since December 1980, when the new Foreign Exchange and Foreign Trade Control Law was implemented (Feldman 1986; Ito 1983, 1986; Mutoh and Hamada 1984; Otani and Tiwari 1981). In addition, the differential between the gensaki and Euroyen interest rates is now very small. It has been suggested that the presence of capital controls in Japan was the main reason why covered interest rate parity did not hold before 1980, despite apparent arbitrage possibilities. Hence, barriers to the inflow and outflow of short term funds appear to have been significantly reduced by the 1980 law.

The examination by Pettway and Tapley (1985) of the prices and returns of some dually listed stock on the Tokyo and New York stock exchanges suggests that, far from being segmented from the rest of the world, the Tokyo stockmarket is fairly well integrated with the rest of the world (or at least with the New York exchange). This conclusion is reinforced by the fact that Japanese stockmarkets also suffered in the crash of October 1987. The recent entry of foreign securities companies into the Tokyo Stock Exchange and the movement of Japanese securities companies abroad can be expected to accelerate this integration.

Asset substitutability must be distinguished from capital mobility. Even if capital is very mobile across national borders, assets of the same maturity denominated in different currencies may not be perfect substitutes. Whether bonds of the same maturity denominated in different currencies are perfect substitutes is indicated by whether uncovered interest rate parity holds. With respect to uncovered interest rate parity for three-month yen and dollar assets,

Ito's (1986) results suggest that uncovered interest rate parity has held since 1977; this is notwithstanding the fact that capital controls were sufficient to prevent covered interest rate parity from holding in the early period of his study.

More recent research questions this finding, and provides evidence for the hypothesis that short term yen and dollar assets are still imperfect substitutes for one another (McKenzie 1986; Takeuchi and Yamamoto 1987). It is theoretically possible that the substitutability between assets denominated in yen and those denominated in other currencies increases as capital controls are eliminated, but these studies cannot indicate whether the degree of substitutability between these assets has in fact increased over time.

One consequence of financial deregulation and the internationalisation of financial markets is that the variety of assets available to investors is widened. This poses problems concerning the definition and controllability of the money supply (see, for example, Argy 1989). Should foreign currency deposits held by residents and yen-denominated deposits held by non-residents be included in the monetary aggregate used for targeting? In fact, for many years Japan has included in its monetary target resident holdings of foreign currency deposits held with banks in Japan and also non-resident holdings of yen deposits with banks in Japan, even though both are rather small and comparatively stable.

The importance of currency substitution—that is, substitution between domestic money and foreign currency money (or bonds)—both generally and as a consequence of financial deregulation, has been widely debated. McKinnon (1982) suggests that the demand for money should be destabilised by currency substitution. Since December 1980, when Japanese corporations and individuals were given permission to hold foreign currency deposits, the possibilities for currency substitution have increased. It is true that studies investigating the demand for money in Japan do not suggest that the Japanese have engaged in significant currency substitution since 1980 (Horiuchi 1987; McKenzie 1986); but this may change over time, particularly with the development of the Tokyo offshore market. However, given that large denomination deposit and lending rates in Japan have been virtually deregulated, Euroyen markets (or the Tokyo offshore market) are unlikely to frustrate domestic monetary policy (Argy 1989).

Real interest rate parity holds if real interest rates across countries are equalised. Should real interest rate parity hold, domestic monetary policy will be powerless unless a country is large enough to influence the 'world' real interest rate. According to Fukao and Hanazaki (1987), there are significant differences between the real interest rate in Japan and the real interest rates in the United States, the United Kingdom, Canada and Australia (but not West Germany). They note that, despite these differences, the average disparity in real interest rates decreased between the periods 1973–80 and 1981–85, a result they attribute to the recent deregulation of exchange controls in a number of countries. This suggests that there is a tendency for real interest rates to converge.

Since forward contracts are typically not available for terms longer than one year, tests of covered interest rate parity for long term assets cannot be implemented to determine the extent to which capital controls impede long term capital flows. Instead, models explaining long term interest rates or capital flows can be used. Fukao and Okubo (1984) find that international factors are becoming more important in explaining long term interest rates in Japan as time goes by, a development that they ascribe to the deregulation of international capital flows.

Some researchers have used estimates of capital-flow equations or equations for the demand for yen-denominated assets with dummy variables to determine the impact of the regulatory changes. Danker (1983) found that the change permitting foreigners to participate in the gensaki and certificate of deposit markets in 1979 did not have a significant impact on the demand by foreigners for yen-denominated assets. However, he did find a significant upward shift in foreign demand for yen-denominated bonds in March 1980. The shift may have reflected anticipations about the implementation of the new foreign exchange law in December 1980; changes in the administration of the existing foreign exchange law; or the inflow of capital from middle eastern countries as a result of an investment mission from those countries to Japan.[1] Fujii and Ueda's (1986) econometric analysis of capital flows suggests that financial liberalisation, the relaxation of restrictions on holding foreign securities, and an increased interest sensitivity by both households and firms have all been factors in increasing Japanese capital outflows in the 1980s.

The possible exchange rate effects resulting from freeing interest rate controls on deposits and deregulation induced shifts from yen bonds to foreign bonds and from yen money to foreign bonds have been discussed in a theoretical way in a number of papers (Argy 1987a; Feldman 1986; Frankel 1984; McKenzie 1986). Eken (1984), in one of the few empirical studies of this issue, estimated equations explaining movements of the real dollar–yen exchange rate. He found that exchange controls encouraging outflows and discouraging inflows contributed to a weaker yen, and that controls encouraging inflows and discouraging outflows contributed to a stronger yen. However, little other empirical evidence on the impact of financial deregulation on the yen–dollar exchange rate is available. This reflects to some extent the difficulties in estimating satisfactory exchange rate equations.

Taxation

The taxation of interest on personal savings has been an issue in Japanese financial deregulation for some time because of its potential impact on the distribution of personal savings among financial institutions and its alleged impact on Japanese saving.

The preferential treatment of small savings by the Japanese tax system is well known. Until 1988, it operated in four principal areas: the non-taxation of interest on small savings on a principal amount up to ¥3 million (maruyu system); the special tax exemption for interest from small government bonds on a principal amount up to ¥3 million (maru-toku system); the tax exemption on interest from postal savings on a principal amount up to ¥3 million; and the system to promote the accumulation of financial assets by wage earners (maru-zai system) to the value of ¥5 million. In addition, capital gains on land, housing and shares are largely tax-free. Lax enforcement of the limits on the number of postal savings accounts and the balances in these accounts held by an individual is widely believed to have encouraged the flow of funds into the postal savings system. Substantial changes in the procedures for proof of identification when opening new accounts were implemented in early 1986, and are expected to have eliminated much of the earlier abuse of the system.

As part of its current tax reform program, the Japanese government has substantially scaled back this preferential tax system by abolishing the tax exemption for interest on small savings and postal savings from April 1988 (except for certain disadvantaged groups) and introducing a 20 per cent withholding tax on interest income. These tax exemptions have been suggested as one of the main reasons for Japan's high savings rate, and as a contributing factor towards Japan's persistent current account surplus. If this is true, the tax changes will induce significant changes in both the pattern of savings and the distribution of savings among financial institutions; but there is currently no convincing evidence that the Japanese interest rate (nominal or real, before tax or after) significantly affects savings (Horioka 1990; McKenzie 1986: 139–41).

Horioka's study (1986) detailing the factors contributing to Japan's high private savings rate (compared with that of the United States) points to the importance of demographic and life-cycle factors in explaining the difference between the two countries in savings rates in the 1970s and 1980s. The most important factor, he suggests, is Japan's relatively low ratio of retired people to working people, which accounts for 11.5 percentage points of Japan's higher savings rate. Horioka also suggests that taxation incentives explain little of the difference in savings rates, and that changes in the tax system are unlikely to have much effect on savings rates. The same reasoning suggests that the liberalisation of interest rates on small-denomination deposits would not greatly influence Japanese savings, but that there could be major effects on the structure of intermediation.

In this chapter some of the broad trends in Japanese financial deregulation have been outlined. First, a significant relaxation of interest rate controls has occurred. Second, there have been substantial regulatory changes in capital flows, with covered interest rate parity now holding, some integration between the Tokyo and New York stock exchanges taking place, and long term capital flows also being influenced.

In a number of significant areas little has changed. Interest rates on small-denomination deposits remain controlled, and relaxing these controls poses a number of critical problems for administrators concerning what should be done about the postal savings system and its relationship with the rest of the financial system. The distinctions between banking and securities business, and between short term and long term banking on the liability side remain broadly intact. Despite the Bank of Japan's best efforts, the treasury bill market still remains undeveloped. In each of these areas inter-Ministry or intra-Ministry conflicts over the direction of deregulation are likely to mean that future deregulation will be slow and piecemeal.

3 Japanese financial markets and the implementation of monetary policy: a retrospective view

Ryuichiro Tachi

In order to assess the impact of developments in the Japanese financial markets in the 1980s, this chapter briefly reviews the important characteristics of the Japanese economic and financial system that prevailed from 1952–53 to 1975. Some of the changes in the system after 1975 are then discussed, together with the main forces that brought them about. Finally, some of the resulting changes in the implementation of monetary policy are outlined.

Japanese finance until 1975

There were five characteristic features of the postwar Japanese financial system: the excess investment economy; the reliance of enterprises on external sources of funds; excess demand in the loan market; steady borrowings by ordinary banks from the Bank of Japan; and segmentation of the financial market and artificial determination of interest rates. Each of these characteristics is discussed briefly below, as is the implementation of monetary policy through window guidance and movements in the call rate.

The Japanese economy of that time was of the excess investment type, where domestic demand exceeded domestic supply and the current account (mainly the trade account) was always in deficit. To prevent a decline in the level of foreign exchange reserves, the monetary authorities took extensive steps to control capital inflows and outflows, and also adopted measures to foster export industries as well as import-competing industries. However, views are divided on the effectiveness of the export promotion policy.

Japanese corporations were obliged to rely on external sources of funds to fill the gap created by the inadequacy of their accumulated funds to meet their investment needs. Most corporate fund financing was met by loans from financial institutions, mainly banks. This phenomenon is called corporate overborrowing.

Due to inflation in the immediate postwar period, the real value of the

45

accumulated funds of financial institutions declined substantially. As a result, demand exceeded supply in the loan market, creating a state of excess demand. The shortfall was raised through the interbank call market,[1] but ultimately in the form of loans from the Bank of Japan.

Some of the loanable funds were therefore supplied by the Bank of Japan, but the amount of lending remained within the limits of the amount required for the right cash supply for economic growth. Hence the maximum lending rate was regulated to prevent the rise in the lending rate that would otherwise have occurred, and credit rationing was implemented.

It is believed that steady borrowings by ordinary banks from the Bank of Japan arose because these banks were lending in response to corporate requirements for long term funds. This is against the principle of 'sound banking'. For this reason the financial system was reformed in 1952–53, when the long term credit banks, the trust banks and the banks specialising in financial services for small and medium sized corporations were established. Coupled with the separation of banking and securities business under the Securities and Exchange Law of 1947, this reform established the principle of the division of labour in the area of finance. Nevertheless, mixed banking still exists, in that Japanese ordinary banks also serve as savings banks.

With this division of labour, the Japanese financial market became compartmentalised and interest rates were determined artificially for individual markets. Arbitrage between different markets was seldom facilitated. Such conditions were maintained for a long time. The official discount rate was used as a base rate to determine interest rates on ordinary deposits and time deposits, and the short term prime rate. In addition, using the rate on bank debentures as a base rate, the rates on loans in trust, the terms of issues of public and corporate bonds and the long-term prime rate were decided under administrative guidance. In fact, the terms of issues of public and corporate bonds were set irrespective of the yields of the same bonds in the secondary market.

This interest rate structure was based on the administration's principles of setting long term interest rates higher than short term interest rates, and setting the credit rating of the public sector higher than that of the private sector. Accordingly, the financial system was so designed that, if short term money was borrowed and then lent out on a long term basis, a profit was a virtual certainty provided there was no default.

As Japan's economy grew, physical assets and financial resources accumulated, bringing about changes to this system. Lending rates were liberalised fairly early. As for deposit rates, while liberalisation of the interest rates on certificates of deposit and large-denomination savings deposits progressed, small-denomination deposit rates remain regulated to this day. The trend towards homogeneity in financial institutions is rapidly becoming established while the traditional system remains in place.

Thus the Japanese financial system was what Hicks (1974) terms an 'overdraft economy', where corporations kept no 'liquid reserves' and had to depend entirely on banks for liquidity. Similarly, monetary policy in these circumstances influenced direct investment, corporate production and investment, not through the price mechanism, as assumed by traditional monetary theories (that is, interest rate changes) but through changes in lending by financial institutions. In other words, the Bank of Japan, through changes in its lending attitude towards the private banks, through buying and selling securities, and through the 'discount window', influenced the call rate, the only floating rate in the interest rate regime at that time. Fluctuations in the call rate are considered to affect the lending attitudes of commercial banks, thus causing shifts in the loan supply curve and in the amount of lending. This ultimately helps to cause rises or falls in inventory adjustment and equipment investment.

Since these adjustments through the call rate take time to occur, the Bank of Japan often takes the step of directly controlling the lending of private financial institutions. This is what is called window guidance. Later, it was called the credit ceiling system. But it stands for a kind of moral suasion which does not aim to penalise the parties in cases where the rules are not observed. For this reason some people question the effectiveness of window guidance, but in my view it gave the Bank of Japan the title and the role of lender of last resort.

One of the points of dispute about the operation of monetary policy in Japan before 1975 has been which was more effective, window guidance or fluctuations in the call rates.

Another point concerned the allocation of funds by quota in the loanable funds market. As I noted earlier, to prevent interest rate rises the upper limits of interest rates, including deposit rates and lending rates, are regulated in Japan. This causes excess demand for loanable funds in the loanable funds market. Funds are therefore allocated to each sector by quota. Monetary policy, whether through the Bank of Japan's lending attitude or through its window guidance, ultimately affects overall economic activity by influencing the loan supply curve. This is a widely held view. In their study following Jaffee and Modigliani (1969), Kaizuka and Onodera (1974) showed that in Japan credit rationing exists not as 'equilibrium credit rationing' but as 'dynamic credit rationing'. Dynamic credit rationing arises from the disequilibrium caused by slow adjustment of the market loan rate to its equilibrium level. This slow adjustment results from administrative regulations and other institutional factors.

On the other hand, Kuroda (1979), on the basis of a verification of arbitrage relationships, asserted that there was an arbitrage relationship between the lending rates and the gensaki rates, the latter representing an open market rate. He further verified, using the Sims (1972) test,[2] that there was a one-way causal relationship from gensaki rates to lending rates. This implies that the effective lending rate is determined by market forces. Furukawa (1979), Ito (1985), Ito and Ueda (1981, 1982), Iwata and Hamada (1980), and Ueda (1982), among others, have also tested this hypothesis. These studies support the view that, whether nominal or effective rates are used, there has been upward rigidity of lending rates. This is clear proof of the presence of dynamic credit rationing.

Financial liberalisation and monetary policy

Since 1975 the Japanese financial system has been exposed to drastic changes which have prompted the relaxation or removal of various regulations. This has stimulated adjustments in the functioning of the system, which have led in turn to further liberalisation. Such trends have had an enormous impact on monetary policy, and they are likely to persist in the immediate future.

This chapter next reviews the background to and development of deregulation. The background includes changes in the flow of funds, the accumulation of assets by individuals, and the emergence of the government as a large-scale borrower. The discussion of the development of deregulation is focused on how the loan market, the short term government securities market and the corporate bond market have developed.

First, there were changes in the flow of funds. The decline in the rate of economic growth that accompanied the decrease in investment opportunities within Japan triggered a fall in the share of the corporate sector in the total amount of fund raising. Expansionary fiscal policy to offset the deflationary effects of declining corporate investment led to a massive deficit in the government sector, and the government was obliged to issue government bonds in large quantities. In other words, Japan had shifted from an excess domestic investment type of economy, as described in the previous section, to one characterised by excess domestic savings. Thus the Japanese economy has become one where budget deficits are the norm. Rising current account surpluses have led to rising capital account deficits (excess capital exports). The revised Foreign Exchange Law, which came into force in December 1980, took a step forward in moving from a total ban on international flows of capital to free flows of capital, at least in principle. Emergency powers of control were retained. The legislation was implemented partly in response to criticism from overseas, but it was to be expected in any case as a natural development.

Along with economic growth, the accumulation of financial assets by both individuals and corporations has quickened. Interest preference has also risen, so that investors react quickly even to small changes in after-tax interest rates. Particularly notable in this respect has been the tendency of institutional investors—for example, pension fund and trust fund institutions and life insurance companies—to increase their asset holdings. It cannot be denied that the relaxation of regulations encouraged pension investment, nor that this, with the deregulation of interest rates, has made interest rates very volatile.

Because the government became a major entity in fund raising (together with corporate entities), and because bank borrowings lack marketability (transferability), government bonds, with their inherent marketability, came to be issued in bulk. Consequently, Japan's financial markets were made more secure. To promote the smooth sale of large quantities of government bonds, the implicit quota restrictions on the sale of bonds by financial institutions were relaxed in 1977. This gave way to the formation of a market for free dealing in public and corporate bonds, with an ensuing deregulation of government bond yields. Similarly, the terms of issue of government bonds have acquired some flexibility, and steps have been taken towards public tenders for government bonds. Hence financial deregulation has made rapid progress.

In 1980, with a view to preventing a fall in government bond prices and accelerating their sales, investment trust funds and government bond funds were established.[3] The sums deposited in these funds are invested in medium term government bonds. These funds were well received by investors. Their innovative nature helped to boost their shares in the market, and other financial institutions have faced the urgent need to match them with competitive assets with unregulated interest rates.

With regulated interest rates it is still the conventional practice to determine the short term prime rate at a fixed margin above the official discount rate, and the long term rate at a fixed margin above the subscriber yield on bank debentures. These rates in turn serve as the basic loan rates of government financial institutions. However, along with the changes in the underlying trends described earlier, the emphasis in the process of deregulation has shifted to deposit rates.

Dynamic credit rationing has hardly grown at all. Credit rationing was not completely eliminated even after 1975; but it was no longer brought about by adjustment delays arising from administrative regulations or other institutional factors. Rather, credit rationing corresponded to the 'equilibrium credit rationing' discussed by Jaffee and Modigliani (1969).

Takenaka (1983) attempted to trace changes in the adjustment speed of loan interest rates to changes in official interest rates.[4] He concluded that adjustment to changes in official rates was rather slow until the middle of 1960 but started to speed up gradually thereafter, and that after 1978 adjustment substantially accelerated. Similar results were obtained by the Sumitomo Trust Bank Research Department (Sumitomo Shintaku Ginkō Chōsabu 1985).

These studies made use of Fair and Jaffee's method (1972), but Asako and Uchino (1987) analysed the Japanese loan market using a method that yields more clearcut conclusions. They found that the disequilibrium in Japan's postwar loan market had been brought about not by the delay in interest rate adjustment but by such factors as the policy oriented artificial basing of loan rates on the official discount rate. This supports the validity of the 'policy interest rate hypothesis'—a hypothesis which suggests that disequilibrium in the loans market originates from the policy determined loans rate, which is not necessarily set to achieve equilibrium. They also concluded that the evidence supporting the hypothesis is stronger the more recent the data used.

The proposition that there is disequilibrium in the loan market, and that it is caused by policy oriented factors, is a firm ground for our claim. However, the argument that the more recent the period of measurement the stronger the evidence supporting the policy based interest rate hypothesis is directly opposed to our observation. In all probability this is because since 1980 the meaning of the policy based interest rate itself has changed. The extent of credit rationing has declined considerably since 1975. This is mainly because of the globalisation of finance; in particular, the means of fund raising have diversified and alternative means of fund raising are being used (for example, convertible bonds) that have increased interest arbitrage and accelerated market restructuring.

The loan market itself is a negotiated market, where loans lack the transferability of securities. On the other hand, in this market both financial institutions and borrowers can benefit by fixing loan rates in a tacit agreement to share the risks caused by fluctuations in interest rates. So credit rationing with fixed rates in the loan market is possible, even if interest rates are deregulated. The prospect that such credit rationing (equilibrium rationing) will continue cannot be denied—a point that is stressed by Ikeo (1985) and Osano and Tsutsui (1985).

As I mentioned earlier, past regulatory policies persist in that short term and long term prime rates are determined on the bases of the official discount rate and the yields on interest bearing bank debentures respectively; but in substance these rates remain nominal because few loans are made at these prime rates. As for deposit rates, various steps have been implemented, including the introduction of negotiable certificates of deposit, the liberalisation of interest rates on large-denomination term deposits, the lowering of the minimum unit for large-denomination deposits, and the shortening of the minimum term of unregulated deposits.[5] The deregulation of interest rates on small-denomination deposits remains to be considered.

Short term money markets are closely related to monetary policy. The gensaki market was a natural development, mediating between corporations with surplus funds and securities houses—among others—that are in need of such funds. It was officially approved in 1976 as the first open money market in Japan. Later, in 1979, the issuing of negotiable certificates of deposit was approved, and the full removal of controls on the level of bill rates and call rates took place in the interbank money market. Call rates, which had played a central role in analyses of Japanese finance because they were the only free-market interest rates in postwar Japan, had been subject to various restrictions until then. At long last these restrictions were abolished.

As mentioned earlier, Japan's basic monetary policy has been to influence interest rates in the interbank money market through changes in the official discount rate and through discount window lending control, thus affecting the amount of lending through changes in the portfolio selection behaviour of the banks. But this monetary policy becomes less effective if reliance on the Bank of Japan's ability to control the levels of bill and call rates, and on the response of bank lending to short term rates, weakens the Bank of Japan's influence on the call and bill markets or the influence of the call and bill rates on bank lending.

After 1975, the share of lending in all funds supplied declined, and the supply of funds in the form of transferable and marketable securities increased in its place. Concurrently, corporate fund raising funds were supplied in the form of interest bearing debentures, convertible bonds and stocks instead of borrowings. Thus, fund raising through securities expanded its share in the total. It has therefore become more difficult than in the past to affect bank credit by manipulating interbank rates so as to influence economic activity; it is now necessary to influence interest rates directly in the open market, thus causing medium and long term interest rates to change.

The principal open money markets in Japan are the gensaki and certificate of deposit markets; but many voices are insisting on the need for a market for government bills (short term government securities) with deregulated interest rates.

Under various laws, the issuing of eight kinds of short term Japanese government bills is approved. Of these eight, those actually issued include treasury bills (okurashō shōken), food bills (shokuryō shōken) and foreign exchange fund bills (gaikoku kawase shikin shōken).[6] Treasury bills in Japan differ slightly from United States treasury bills. Unlike government bonds, Japanese treasury bills are issued to cover a temporary shortage of funds arising from a gap between revenue and expenditure, and are, in principle, redeemable within the fiscal year of issue. In other words, while treasury bills in the United States, except for their term, do not differ from government bonds, Japanese treasury bills must in principle be redeemable within the fiscal year of issue. Other government bills—for example, food bills—are also temporary. Treasury bills, because of their nature, were permitted to be issued even when there was a balanced budget.

Since 1956, treasury bills in Japan have been issued by offering a fixed percentage to the public on specific terms. If the amount subscribed does not reach the expected level, the Bank of Japan takes up the balance. In effect, however, because the interest rate on treasury bills is set lower than the market yield, treasury bills are issued with the Bank of Japan acting as underwriter: most treasury bill holdings are shared between the Bank of Japan, the Trust Fund Bureau (which purchases treasury bills with its surplus funds), government accounts (for instance, the National Debt Consolidation Fund Special Account), and government financial institutions (such as the Japan Development Bank), with the private sector holding the remaining small portion.[7] Hitherto, therefore, issuing treasury bills has not been very different from borrowing from the Bank of Japan.

Nevertheless, treasury bills have their merits: they have a high credit rating and a much greater lot size than bank certificates of deposit, for example, which makes them much more attractive as a trading commodity. And they are not subject to the restrictions imposed on the gensaki market, so the creation of an open market where treasury bills can play a central role can be justified.

In May 1981 the Bank of Japan, to increase its market intervention instruments, began to sell treasury bills to commercial banks as a way of absorbing surplus funds in financial markets. Today, accumulated sales of treasury bills have reached a substantial level. These sales are not by public tender; the terms and conditions are determined by the bill rates and the gensaki rates.

Treasury bills are considered an attractive instrument for fund investment, and have also been well received by corporations. To create a market where treasury bills may be bought and sold, as they are in Great Britain and the United States, holding entities themselves must grow and their trading must expand. For that purpose, and especially for the purpose of smooth trading operations (without wide fluctuations in interest rates), there must be a substantial number of treasury bills in the market at all times. Quite apart from the thinking of the fiscal authorities, who are naturally reluctant to bear the increased interest burden, it is an issue for immediate study whether it is appropriate to use treasury bills, which were originally designed to smooth the impact of fiscal policy on financial markets, for the implementation of monetary policy.

The new edition of *The Japanese Financial System*, published by the Bank of Japan's Institute of Monetary and Economic Studies, says:

> The Bank of Japan has sold some of these TBs [treasury bills] at market prices in an attempt to foster the growth of a secondary bills market, but a TB market in the true sense of the word has yet to form. Nevertheless, due to the character of the financial assets that would be traded in a Government bill market (that is, their creditworthiness, liquidity, and amount of issue), such a market would be the most appropriate place for the Bank of Japan to carry out monetary policy. For this reason, it is expected that there will be concerted efforts to foster and to develop this market. (Suzuki 1987: 111)

Two short term money markets have recently been established. A yen-denominated bankers' acceptance market was established in June 1985; and a commercial paper market in November 1987. But if large corporations and financial institutions come to rely increasingly on these markets to raise and invest funds, as is the case in the United States and the United Kingdom, Japan's financial markets will change radically.

The regulation of corporate bond issues has continued. For example, eligibility criteria have been used as a means of regulation for companies issuing corporate bonds. The trend towards flexibility and liberalisation has progressed steadily in the floating of bonds in domestic markets, as a result of the rapid deregulation of the flotation of bonds in the Euromarket by domestic corporations. It appears that Japanese corporations will soon be able to procure funds under very favourable conditions in both offshore and onshore markets, and will be able to invest surplus funds to their best advantage.

Financial institutions are quite rapidly increasing the shares of unregulated certificates of deposit, commercial paper and commercial bills in the total funds raised, and this trend is likely to continue.

Monetary policy

The first objective of Japan's monetary policy after the second world war was to manipulate the supply of funds so as to keep the balance of payments in surplus while preventing the resurgence of inflation. But when soaring prices followed the first oil crisis (1973–74) the top priority became price stabilisation. To achieve this, the traditional policy of emphasising lending by financial institutions was replaced by a concentration on the rate of growth of the money supply, in particular M2 + CD,[8] as an intermediate goal. The policy adopted by the Bank of Japan for controlling M2 + CD was in principle the same as it had been in the past: that is, to regulate lending to the banking sector through the 'discount window', and to influence interbank market rates, as well as lending by financial institutions, through buying and selling bills (bill operation). Since 1975, however, securities operations by the Bank of Japan and the Sinking Fund have gradually grown in importance. Institutionally, there was a shift after 1975 from allocating a quota of the amount of securities to be purchased by financial institutions to a new formula of tender by negotiation.

Through these policy measures, Japan controlled its money supply and stabilised prices as well. One reason for this success was that, while substitutability among various types of financial assets has recently developed and new commodities, such as money market certificates, have been introduced, substitutability between money and other types of assets is still low. This is because the liberalisation of Japan's capital and financial markets was slow compared with that of the United States. If the interest rate determined in the free market is paid on money, it is immaterial whether assets are held in money or in other forms, so that what is to be controlled cannot be readily identified. Japan has the good fortune to be exempt from this difficulty. To put it in Poole's (1970) terms, the money demand function in Japan is relatively stable, and the disturbances during this period mainly came not from the monetary side of the economy but from the real side, such as the oil crises; that is, through changes in relative prices.[9]

Second, the intentions of the monetary authorities, including the Bank of Japan, were recognised by the Japanese public, and the policy was perceived as credible. In other words, the growth of the money supply never deviated much from public expectations. This has helped to increase the public's trust in the monetary policy and the rapid and unexpected stabilisation of prices that it promoted. This stabilisation was partly due to United States monetary and fiscal policy, and gave rise to Japan's massive external current account surplus and internal fiscal deficit.

Faced with this current account surplus, monetary policy in Japan is turning from its traditional objective of price stabilisation alone to the new goal of emphasising both the exchange rate and prices. The major countries' prosecution of their own policies under the floating exchange rate system —the United States budget deficit and the pursuit of price stability by West Germany and Japan—has been partly responsible for international disequilibrium. In the interest of international collaboration, the monetary policy stance of Japan from now on must include consideration of exchange rates as well as prices.

With the continuing deregulation of finance and the internationalisation of the yen, securitisation of finance will advance and the share of lending in total intermediation will decrease, while the substitutability between financial assets will increase. This will undoubtedly have a substantial impact not only on the stability of finance but also on the effectiveness of monetary policy.

It remains to reiterate that, following Japan's shift from a financial system centred on lending without transferability to a system centred on marketable assets (like those of the United Kingdom and the United States), Japan will soon be facing the problem that is disturbing the United States today—that is, that the money supply itself may be beyond control.

4 Japanese corporate finance and behaviour: recent developments and the impact of deregulation

Paul Sheard

In recent years, significant changes have occurred in the nature of corporate finance in Japan. In terms of both procuring and using funds, Japanese corporate finance has become more diversified, more internationalised, and more sophisticated. Commentators have coined such terms as 'securitisation' (shōkenka) and 'zai-tech' (zaiteku) to describe these trends. These developments have been stimulated largely by regulatory changes, but they have also given an impetus to deregulation itself.

This chapter has two aims. The first is to survey recent developments in Japanese corporate finance and the second is to discuss the implications of these developments, and of the ongoing deregulation of the Japanese financial system, for the micro-level organisation of the capital market. 'Micro-level organisation' means such matters as how the capital market produces and disseminates information; how it assesses and reallocates risks; how it monitors the performance of corporate assets and reorganises them when necessary; and how it copes with the problems of incentives associated with asymmetries in the availability of information and the delegation of tasks among agents in the capital market (for example, between security holders and managers).

One common notion is that the functioning of competitive markets tends to solve any informational and incentive problems associated with the operation on the microeconomic level of the capital market. This is the idea that information will be supplied to the market through such devices as bond-rating agencies, securities analysts, investment advisors and financial consultants, and that a competitive takeover market will ensure that managers act in the interests of shareholders.

These sorts of institutions, however, are notably absent from or underdeveloped in the Japanese capital market—or at least this has been the case in the past. Until recently there were no bond-rating agencies in Japan, and hostile takeover bids are almost unheard of. In Japan a rather different kind of capital market organisation has existed, one in which the informational, risk bearing and corporate control functions have been mostly performed by the principal commercial banks. This is the so-called 'main-bank system' (mein banku sei). An analysis of how this system operates and how it might change in response to financial deregulation forms the main part of this chapter.

Recent developments in corporate finance

Japanese corporate finance in the high growth period was characterised by the 'indirect financing system' (kansetsu kin'yū seido): large firms relied heavily on external sources of finance, and particularly on bank borrowings, whereas stocks and bonds were relatively unimportant.[1] That is, the massive allocation of capital funds from the household to the corporate sector took place through the banking sector, and involved predominantly loan markets rather than stock and bond markets.

In recent years, particularly since the early 1980s, there have been some important changes in the nature of Japanese corporate financing practices (Chōsa, 1986; Ōkurashō Zaisei Kin'yū Kenkyūsho Kenkyūbu 1987). To summarise, there has been: a substantial increase in reliance on internal rather than external sources of funds; a decline in the importance of borrowings as a source of external finance and a rise in that of stocks and bonds, particularly equity-linked bonds; within borrowings, an increase in the relative importance of short term as opposed to long term borrowings; a dramatic increase in the proportion of total securities issued overseas; and a trend towards greater emphasis by firms on the efficient management of financial resources.

In the early 1970s, 33 per cent of the net increase in funds procured by Japanese corporations came from internal sources and 53 per cent came from external sources; by the early 1980s the share of internal sources had risen to 48 per cent and that of external sources had fallen to 45 per cent (Tamura 1987: 3). For listed firms this change was much more pronounced: internal sources provided 36 per cent of net increases in funds in the early 1970s, but this had increased to 71 per cent by the early 1980s, with the share of external sources falling from 51 per cent to 29 per cent (Tamura 1987: 11).

In the early 1970s, 41 per cent of the net increase in funds available to listed firms was in the form of bank borrowings, but by the mid-1980s this had fallen to 6 per cent. The share of stocks and bonds, on the other hand, rose from 10 per cent to 23 per cent. It is worth noting, however, that this trend was much less pronounced for the corporate sector as a whole, reflecting the fact that the changes are occurring mainly in the large (listed firm) corporate sector. For all corporations, the contribution of bank borrowings to the net increment in funds obtained declined slightly, from 47 per cent in the early 1970s to 37 per cent in the mid-1980s, while the contribution of stocks and bonds increased only marginally, from 6 per cent to 8 per cent (Tamura 1987: 3).

The most dramatic decline has been in the share of long term borrowings. In the early 1970s long term borrowings accounted for 23 per cent of the net increase in funds procured by listed firms (the largest single source), but by

Table 4.1 Trends in overseas bond issues by Japanese firms, 1965–87 (billion yen)

	Straight bonds	Convertible bonds	Warrant bonds	Total
1965	—	—	—	—
1966	—	—	—	—
1967	3.6	5.4	—	9.0
1968	39.6	10.8	—	50.4
1969	20.2	46.4	—	66.6
1970	—	16.2	—	16.2
1971	9.8	—	—	9.8
1972	—	—	—	—
1973	5.4	—	—	5.4
1974	102.2	20.3	—	122.5
1975	293.0	182.0	—	475.0
1976	213.5	153.8	—	367.3
1977	146.5	221.1	—	367.6
1978	127.0	428.1	—	555.1
1979	178.6	556.1	—	734.7
1980	168.0	514.9	—	682.9
1981	49.1	1,024.8	44.3	1,118.2
1982	681.2	627.5	65.8	1,374.5
1983	403.9	1,191.4	323.1	1,918.4
1984	1,134.5	1,227.2	433.5	2,795.2
1985	1,439.3	948.0	866.2	3,253.5
1986	1.639.2	485.3	1,993.2	4,117.7
1987	824.0	1,076.6	3,439.0	5,339.6
(per cent)	(15.4)	(20.0)	(64.4)	(100.0)

Primary source: Ministry of Finance (Japan) Ōkurashō Shōken Kyoku Nenpō (Annual Report of the Securities Bureau).

Source: Kuroda (1987: 12). For 1985–87, constructed from Table 114 in Ministry of Finance (Japan) Ōkurashō Shōken Kyoku Nenpō (Annual Report of the Securities Bureau) (1988).

the early 1980s the absolute level of long term borrowings was falling and the contribution of long term borrowings to the net increase in funds procured was negative. For large firms with ¥1 billion or more in capital these trends are particularly evident, with the proportion of bonds and shares in the net increase in external funds rising from 26 per cent in 1975 to 66 per cent in 1984 and the level of long term borrowings outstanding beginning to fall sharply from 1983 (Ōkurashō Zaisei Kin'yū Kenkyūsho Kenkyūbu 1987: 83).

The internationalisation of Japanese corporate finance has accelerated since the amendment of the Foreign Exchange and Foreign Trade Control Law in 1980 (table 4.1), and has centred on issues of convertible and warrant bonds in the Swiss and Eurodollar bond markets (table 4.2). In the late 1970s, 19 per cent of the funds raised from issues of stocks and bonds came from overseas, but by the mid-1980s half of these funds were coming from overseas (table 4.3). In 1984 the amount of straight bonds issued overseas exceeded the

Table 4.2 Fund procurement by Japanese firms through overseas bonds, 1977–88 (US$ million)

	1977	1978	1979	1980	1981	1982	1983	1984	1985	1986	1987	1988
United States												
No. of issues	5	5	1	1	5	4	3	6	1	—	5	7
Amount	381	139	80	60	350	325	52.2	450.5	200	—	712	1,175
per cent	18.6	5.0	1.9	1.6	7.4	5.2	0.4	3.0	1.0	0.0	1.7	2.5
Eurodollar												
No. of issues	35	11	15	25	50	40	50	110	156	202	227	239
Amount	940	405	640	930	2,060	1,908.7	3,923.9	8,182.3	11,425	16,340	25,817	32,415
per cent	45.8	14.6	15.2	25.4	43.4	30.3	35.0	54.2	55.2	56.4	61.1	68.7
Deutschmark												
No. of issues	9	36	18	12	3	10	14	16	21	17	10	20
Amount	245.1	1,110.8	730.4	534.6	120.2	241.4	491.3	504.1	758.8	982.7	780.8	1,502.6
per cent	12.0	39.7	17.4	14.6	2.5	3.8	4.4	3.3	3.7	3.4	1.9	3.2
Swiss franc												
No. of issues	19	46	106	73	65	133	230	205	222	204	1	181
Amount	484.7	1,129.8	2,714.1	1,942.7	1,831.4	3,631.3	6,543.9	5,601.8	6,079.0	7,889.8	8,993.9	9,784.9
per cent	23.6	40.7	64.6	53.0	38.5	57.6	58.2	37.1	29.4	27.2	21.3	20.7
Other												
No. of issues	—	—	1	7	10	5	6	8	45	44	49	41
Amount	—	—	36.3	196.8	388.0	196.7	224.0	355.1	2,249.2	3,754.3	5,887.4	2,285.7
per cent	—	—	0.9	5.4	8.2	3.1	2.0	2.4	10.9	13.0	13.9	4.8
Total												
No. of issues	68	98	141	118	133	192	303	345	445	467	476	488
Amount	2,050.8	2,774.6	4,200.8	3,664.1	4,749.6	6,303.1	11,235.3	15,093.8	20,712.0	28,966.8	42,191.1	47,163.2
per cent	100.0	100.0	100.0	100.0	100.0	100.0	100.0	100.0	100.0	100.0	100.0	100.0
Private sector												
No. of issues	63	95	138	110	124	175	284	323	427	450	419	488
Amount	1,668.3	2,725.9	3,996.6	3,228.2	4,319.5	5,381.6	10,122.5	13,561.7	19,379.4	27,281.3	40,755.6	47,163.2
Proportion of total (per cent)	81.3	98.2	95.1	88.1	90.9	85.4	91.0	89.9	93.6	94.2	96.6	100.0

Note: Data include bonds issued by overseas subsidiaries under guarantee from a Japanese parent firm, and government guaranteed bonds.
Primary source: Ministry of Finance (Japan) *Kokusai Kin'yū Kyoku Nenpō* (Annual Report of the International Finance Bureau).
Source: Ōkurashō Zaisei Kin'yū Kenkyūsho Kenkyūbu, 1987, pp. 86–87.
For 1985–88, constructed from Tables 38 and 42 in Ministry of Finance (Japan) *Kokusai Kin'yū Kyoku Nenpō* (Annual Report of the International Finance Bureau) (1989).

Table 4.3 Sources of funds for Japanese companies by kind of security issued, 1975–87 (billion yen)

	1975–79 (average)	1980	1981	1982	1983	1984	1985	1986	1987
Shares									
Domestic									
issues at par value	314.0	155.7	475.1	154.0	61.9	38.5	33.3	14.8	2.5
issues at between market price and par value	1.9	20.4	5.6	31.4	79.6	31.1	153.3	104.9	475.5
issues at market price	473.7	906.3	1,279.9	805.9	556.9	710.7	347.5	474.1	1,494.6
third party issues	36.1	77.7	32.6	24.1	151.1	34.5	27.2	37.7	111.3
(Sub-total)	825.7	1,160.1	1,793.2	1,015.4	849.5	814.8	651.3	631.5	2,083.9
Overseas (depository receipts)	40.3	115.3	280.0	62.6	77.8	49.4	10.7	0.6	39.0
Sub-total	866.0	1,275.4	2,073.2	1,078.0	927.3	864.2	662.0	632.1	2,112.9
Straight bonds									
Domestic	1,304.6	993.5	1,269.0	1,047.5	683.0	720.0	943.5	980.0	915.0
Overseas	199.9	213.8	52.3	681.2	403.9	1,134.5	1,493.3	1,639.2	824.0
Sub-total	1,504.5	1,207.3	1,321.3	1,728.7	1,086.9	1,854.5	2,382.8	2,619.2	1,739.0
Convertible bonds									
Domestic	235.9	96.5	526.0	417.5	861.0	1,611.5	1,585.5	3,468.0	5,055.0
Overseas	320.0	536.9	1,026.1	627.5	1,191.4	1,227.1	948.0	485.3	1,076.6
Sub-total	555.9	623.4	1,552.1	1,045.0	2,052.4	2,533.5	2,533.5	3,953.3	6,131.6
Warrant bonds									
Domestic	0	0	20.0	47.0	17.0	3.0	55.0	104.0	0.0
Overseas	0	0	43.5	65.8	323.1	433.5	866.2	1,993.2	3,439.0
Sub-total	0	0	63.5	112.8	340.1	436.5	921.2	2,097.2	3,439.0
Total	2,926.4	3,106.1	5,010.1	3,964.5	4,406.7	5,993.8	6,499.5	9,301.8	13,422.5
Overseas fund raising	560.2	856.0	1,401.9	1,437.1	1,996.2	2,844.5	3,264.2	4,118.3	5,378.6
(per cent)	(19.1)	(27.6)	(28.0)	(36.2)	(45.3)	(47.4)	(50.2)	(44.3)	(40.1)

Note: Capital increases include issuance by financial institutions; bonds exclude bank bonds.
Source: Tamura (1987: 8). Figures for 1986 and 1987, together with corrections to some of Tamura's figures, were obtained from Tables 42, 113 and 114 in Ministry of Finance (Japan) *Kokusai Kin'yū Kyoku Nenpō* (Annual Report of the International Finance Bureau) (1988).

amount issued domestically for the first time; and in 1987 the amount of warrant bonds issued overseas was more than triple the amount of domestic straight bond issues. When borrowings are included, by the early 1980s large Japanese firms were raising almost a quarter of their funds in foreign currency, compared with just 1 per cent in the early 1970s (Ōkurashō Zaisei Kin'yū Kenkyūsho Kenkyūbu 1987: 81).

The main-bank system

The internationalisation and 'securitisation' of Japanese corporate finance and the continuing deregulation of Japan's financial system raise some fundamental questions about the organisation of the Japanese capital market at the microeconomic level. Are 'customer-type' markets being supplanted by 'auction-type' markets? Are long term information and risk sharing arrangements between banks and corporate borrowers giving way to spot-market relationships where the price mechanism plays a more direct role? Is the way information is produced and transmitted in the capital market changing? What is happening to 'stable shareholding' arrangements? To what extent will a competitive market for corporate control develop in Japan—that is, an arena where agents bid openly for the right to control corporate assets? In short, what are the implications for the traditional main-bank system?

Much of the literature has focused on Japan's indirect financing system and the associated phenomena of 'overloan' and 'overborrowing' by banks and industrial borrowers respectively (Royama 1984; Suzuki 1980: ch.1). Rather less attention has been paid to the fact that within the context of this indirect financing system a particular form of relationship has existed between banks and corporate borrowers, centring on the main-bank system (Hodder and Tscheogl 1985). The term 'main-bank system' denotes that most large firms in Japan maintain a close relationship with one or more of the major commercial banks.[2] Although the main bank does not have any official or legal status, there is general recognition among financiers, businessmen and regulators concerning which is the 'main' bank for a given firm. The closest thing to a formal definition of a main bank is that it is the (non-government) bank which holds the largest loan share for a firm (typically 10–20 per cent). The main bank is also generally a major shareholder in the firm and has close managerial and informational ties with it, often extending to representation on its board and participation in its management (for more details, see Sheard 1986a).

In economic terms, the main bank performs three closely interrelated functions in the capital market: risk bearing, monitoring, and corporate control. A feature of the main-bank system is that these capital-market services are provided largely in an implicit fashion, or 'internalised', rather than being provided explicitly through market exchange. A key issue is the extent to which changes in Japan's financial system will alter the way these capital-market services are provided, and, in particular, whether more market oriented mechanisms will supplant the main bank system. A related question is whether some elements of the main-bank system will persist while others wane or disappear.

Insurance of corporate risks

As I have noted, the bank regarded by the capital market as the 'main' bank is the one that maintains the largest share in total loans to the firm, bank loans being historically the most important source of funds to corporate borrowers. A peculiar and largely implicit aspect of the main-bank system, however, is that the main bank performs a role in risk bearing vis-à-vis its corporate borrowers that is rather special, and greater than would be suggested by the size of its loan share (or shareholding). In Japanese business thinking, being the main bank carries an implicit responsibility for the welfare and survival of the firm. The main bank is not just the most important bank for the firm in quantitative terms; it carries a special importance in qualitative terms as the bank on which the firm can rely for financial support in times of corporate need. More formally, the relationship between the firm and its main bank is one where the bank insures the firm against some of the risks of corporate downturn and, in the last analysis, against business failure.

There is considerable case study and anecdotal evidence to support the view that the main bank is an implicit insurer for its corporate borrowers (for details, see Nakatani 1984; Sheard 1985). For instance, when banks provide a struggling firm with financial assistance, the main bank commonly assumes a disproportionately large burden, either in terms of direct measures such as providing interest reductions or exemptions, or indirectly in terms of increasing its loan share (and risk) as the position of the firm deteriorates. In the extreme case of bankruptcy or informal reorganisation, the main bank typically absorbs losses far exceeding its loan share.[3] The main bank is also typically the principal underwriting bank for bonds that the firm issues (Aoki and Miyachi 1987: 4; Watanabe 1987: 13), and it has been a common practice for the main bank to buy up outstanding bonds of firms that have failed, again highlighting the role of the main banks in bearing residual risk.[4]

This aspect of main-bank behaviour can be explained in terms of the main bank performing a kind of implicit insurance role for the firm, analogous to that which the firm is believed to perform for workers in the theory of implicit labour contracts.[5] When a firm enters into a main-bank relationship with a particular bank, it is not just obtaining finance from the capital market; it is also purchasing an implicit insurance contract — that in adverse contingencies the bank will provide financial backup. The main bank is willing to provide this insurance because it receives 'premiums' in the form of higher payments from the firm when conditions are favourable. For instance, the firm may pay a higher nominal interest rate on loans; it may maintain a higher level of deposits with the main bank; it may allocate financial business such as foreign exchange and the discounting of bills preferentially to the main bank; or, more generally, it may refrain from fully exploiting the 'favourable' spot-market conditions that arise from time to time.[6]

One interpretation of the trend by large firms towards more sophisticated financial management—zai-tech (literally 'financial technology')—is that firms might be increasingly internalising risk bearing functions that used to be shouldered by the main banks (see Fingleton 1986; Hughes 1987; Iwaki 1987a, 1987b).

Monitoring

An important aspect of the main bank's role is that among capital market participants it assumes the primary responsibility for screening and monitoring the performance of its corporate borrowers. In a financing system where bank loans were the principal instrument for supplying funds, the main-bank system could be conceived as providing an institutional arrangement for the capital market as a whole to economise on screening and monitoring costs.[7] That is, in the context of the indirect financing system, the main-bank system was largely a substitute for the 'missing' bond-rating agencies and securities analysis industry.

It is important to note that, unlike other information-gathering agencies, the main-bank system does not monitor performance in an explicit market setting.[8] First, in the main-bank system the largest creditor (the main bank) also performs the monitoring function. Unlike the bond-rating agency, which markets its informational services, in the main-bank system the principal monitoring agent internalises the informational services because it is also the principal creditor, in terms of having the largest loan share and significant holdings of shares and bonds. The element of voluntary disclosure on the part of the firm is also important.[9] Second, the capital market at large can use the monitoring output of the main bank, in the sense that other agents can use the actions and attitude of the main bank as signals in their dealings with the firm. These signals can be quite direct, as when the main bank announces that it will continue to support an ailing firm; more typically they are indirect, in that a firm normally approaches its main bank before consulting its other bankers on a financial matter.

It is useful to distinguish between two kinds of capital market signalling. Several commentators have emphasised the role of the government owned Japan Development Bank, and of industrial policy more generally, in signalling the government's resource allocation intentions to the private sector:[10] this kind of signalling pertains to the sectoral allocation of resources. The implicit signalling that occurs through the operation of the main-bank system, on the other hand, relates more to the transmission of information about the creditworthiness and prospects of individual firms. To borrow Diamond's (1984) term, the main bank functions as a 'delegated monitor' in the capital market.

Though separable for analytical purposes, the risk bearing and monitoring functions of the main bank are closely related. Because main banks specialise in screening and monitoring corporate borrowers, they acquire information that enhances their capacity to insure corporate risks (by alleviating the problems of moral hazard and adverse selection that plague insurance markets); and because they specialise in risk bearing, they have an incentive to screen and monitor the firms whose risks they choose to bear.

Intervention

The role of the main banks extends beyond screening and monitoring; the main bank also intervenes actively in the management of firms in times of corporate crisis or poor performance. The main-bank system provides a mechanism through which the 'corporate control' function of the capital market is exercised (see Shleifer and Vishny 1986; Stiglitz 1985). Thus the main-bank system is closely related to another distinguishing feature of Japanese capital market organisation: the virtual absence of an external takeover market like those in the United States and Australia. 'Stable shareholding arrangements' between banks and firms militate against the operation of an external market for corporate control, but within this (loosely) internalised capital market the main bank is in effect the agent of 'delegated intervention'. In a sense, the main-bank system substitutes for the 'missing' takeover market.

In the literature, it is argued that competition in the 'market for corporate control' serves to discipline managers and so minimise the agency costs associated with the widespread separation of ownership and control in capitalist economies (Jensen and Ruback 1983; Manne 1965). The takeover market provides a mechanism for the capital market to allocate to competing management teams the rights to manage corporate resources, and, when the managers of a firm are not performing well, to displace them and bring the assets of the firm under more efficient management. In this story, even so-called corporate raiders are seen as performing a socially useful function (Holderness and Sheehan 1985).

This kind of story implicitly assumes a competitive kind of managerial labour market, in that management is assumed to be just another factor of production in the firm, albeit one prone to producing low levels of output in the absence of an appropriate incentive structure. A distinctive feature of the managerial labour market in Japan is that it is highly internalised, and that external managerial labour markets are neither very disaggregated (in terms of professional subgroups) nor very active (in terms of inter-firm mobility through the market). Against this institutional background, the market for corporate control has taken on a particular form in the Japanese capital market.

An active external takeover market has not developed in Japan, largely because of the nature of intercorporate shareholdings.[11] Corporate ownership in Japan is characterised by a high level of corporate ownership of shares (around 70 per cent) (table 4.4) and extensive interlocking among related

Table 4.4 Proportional share ownership of listed Japanese firms by type of shareholder, 1950–87

	Financial institutions	Investment trusts	Securities companies	Non-financial domestic corporations	Sub-total for domestic corporations	Government and public institutions	Japanese individuals and others	Foreign corporations/ individuals	Total (million shares)
1950	12.6	—	11.9	11.0	35.5	3.1	61.3	—	2,581
1951	18.2	—	9.2	13.8	41.2	1.8	57.0	—	3,547
1952	15.8	6.0	8.4	11.8	42.0	1.0	55.8	1.2	5,365
1953	16.3	6.7	7.3	13.5	43.8	0.7	53.8	1.7	7,472
1954	16.7	7.0	7.1	13.0	43.8	0.5	54.0	1.7	9,356
1955	19.5	4.1	7.9	13.2	44.7	0.4	53.2	1.8	11,109
1956	21.7	3.9	7.1	15.7	48.4	0.3	49.9	1.5	16,171
1957	21.4	4.7	5.7	16.3	48.1	0.2	50.1	1.5	19,490
1958	22.4	6.6	4.4	15.8	49.2	0.3	49.1	1.5	22,519
1959	21.7	7.6	3.7	17.3	50.3	0.2	47.8	1.6	27,552
1960	23.1	7.5	3.7	17.8	52.1	0.2	46.3	1.4	34,394
1961	21.3	8.6	2.8	18.7	51.4	0.2	46.7	1.7	50,697
1962	21.5	9.2	2.5	17.7	50.9	0.2	47.1	1.8	62,306
1963	21.4	9.5	2.2	17.9	51.0	0.3	46.7	2.1	70,748
1964	21.6	7.8	4.5	18.4	52.3	0.2	45.6	1.9	81,777
1965	23.3	5.6	5.8	18.4	53.1	0.2	44.8	1.8	83,960
1966	26.1	3.7	5.4	18.6	53.8	0.3	44.1	1.8	87,195

Year									
1967	28.1	2.4	4.4	20.5	55.4	0.3	42.4	1.9	91,856
1968	30.3	1.7	2.1	21.4	55.5	0.3	41.9	2.3	97,784
1969	30.7	1.2	1.4	22.1	55.4	0.3	41.1	3.3	106,894
1970	31.0	1.4	1.2	23.1	56.7	0.2	39.9	3.2	119,142
1971	32.6	1.3	1.5	23.6	59.0	0.3	37.2	3.6	127,588
1972	33.9	1.3	1.8	26.6	63.6	0.2	32.7	3.5	136,932
1973	35.1	1.3	1.5	27.5	65.4	0.2	32.7	2.9	149,538
1974	35.5	1.6	1.3	27.1	65.5	0.2	33.5	2.5	158,728
1975	36.0	1.6	1.4	26.3	65.3	0.2	33.5	2.6	172,474
1976	36.5	1.4	1.4	26.5	65.8	0.2	32.9	2.6	183,074
1977	37.8	2.0	1.5	26.2	67.5	0.2	32.0	2.3	192,885
1978	38.8	2.2	1.8	26.3	69.1	0.2	30.8	2.2	199,064
1979	38.9	1.9	2.0	26.1	68.9	0.2	30.4	2.5	206,786
1980	38.8	1.5	1.7	26.0	68.0	0.2	29.2	4.1	215,973
1981	38.7	1.3	1.7	26.3	68.0	0.2	28.5	4.6	230,677
1982	38.9	1.2	1.8	26.0	67.9	0.2	28.0	5.1	239,415
1983	38.0	1.0	1.9	25.9	66.8	0.2	26.8	6.3	249,204
1984	38.5	1.1	1.9	25.9	67.4	0.2	26.3	6.1	258,164
1985	40.9	1.3	2.0	24.1	68.3	0.8	25.2	5.7	318,182
1986	41.7	1.8	2.5	24.5	70.5	0.9	23.9	4.7	330,596
1987	42.2	2.4	2.5	24.9	72.0	0.8	23.6	3.6	347,772

Note: From 1985, the share ownership levels are calculated using listed shares rather than shares outstanding.
Source: Tōkyō Shōken Torihikisho Chōsabu (various editions); Tōshō Tōkei Nenpō.

firms and financial institutions. More significantly, these shares are held mainly under so-called 'stable shareholding arrangements' (antei kabunushi kōsaku), which provide firms with mutual insulation from external takeover.[12]

The banks themselves figure prominently in these stable shareholding arrangements. At the risk of oversimplification, it could be said that the pervasive practice of interlocking shareholdings, centring on but not limited to identifiable groupings, creates a number of 'internalised' capital markets and a situation where the main financial institutions largely own, and in turn are owned by, their major borrowing firms.[13] Table 4.5 illustrates this by examining the pattern of corporate interlocking among the Sumitomo Bank and its principal shareholders.

In the context of these stable shareholding arrangements, the function of main-bank intervention has been analogous to that of the external takeover market. In their main-bank role the principal commercial banks are often instrumental in facilitating, and sometimes engineering, mergers and other restructuring involving their affiliated borrowers. If a firm is experiencing managerial, financial or structural problems, the main bank typically intervenes by sending in a number of bank officers. Sometimes the bank employs a form of 'crisis management', replacing the existing senior management and embarking on an extensive rationalisation of the firm's management, finance and operations. (For more detail, see Sheard 1985, 1986a.) In many cases, main-bank intervention precipitates a major managerial and financial reorganisation without any formal processes of bankruptcy or takeover. Pascale and Rohlen characterise this process as one where '[the bank puts] the company in a quasi-receivership status, but without any involvement from courts or lawyers' (1983: 229). The point is that one of the supposed effects of a competitive takeover market—the displacement of ineffective management and the improved management of corporate assets—is achieved through the very different mechanism of main-bank intermediation.

Implications of recent changes

The previous sections analysed the principal elements of the main-bank system; this section assesses the implications of financial deregulation for the operation of the system.

It is useful at the outset to distinguish two views on the main-bank system: one treats the main-bank system as largely a product of the regulatory system; the other regards it as having an internal economic logic that, while possibly influenced by the regulatory regime, is nevertheless largely independent of it.

The argument for the first view runs roughly as follows. One effect of the regulated indirect financing system was to encourage reliance on bank borrowings and inhibit the development of a corporate bond market; part of the functional division of labour between financial institutions in this regulated environment involved a few banks assuming responsibility for the monitoring and control (takeover) functions of the capital market. In this view, as main banks these major banks are engaged, at least partly, in providing a public good: the production and dissemination of information about firms and their management and the maintenance of an 'orderly' capital market, in terms of preventing takeovers and bankruptcies. Although the banks incur costs in delivering this public good (fixed monitoring costs and occasional ex post financial losses), these costs are offset by other benefits conferred by the position of the banks in the regulatory system.[14]

The second view sees in the main-bank system a logic independent of the regulatory system: it regards the main-bank system as an institutional arrangement that stems principally from the needs of the banks, firms and managers concerned. In this view, there is a private cost–benefit calculus that sustains the system, and seemingly paradoxical behaviour (such as main banks 'voluntarily' incurring disproportionately large losses) can be rationalised as optimal behaviour in the context of long term organisational equilibrium, taking account of incentive, risk sharing and reputation effects.

It could be argued, for example, that it is the nature of the Japanese managerial employment system rather than financial regulation which lies at the heart of the operation of the main-bank system. Under the lifetime employment system, the welfare of managers is closely tied up with the performance of the firm; and this seems to imply, all other things being equal, that Japanese executives are more threatened by events such as corporate failure or external (hostile) takeover that have bad consequences for the manager's relationship with the firm. The thrust of this chapter is towards the view that the main-bank system reflects optimal arrangements among private actors, but that is not to deny that financial deregulation could have far-reaching ramifications for the operation of the system.

One issue is whether firms will need the same level of 'insurance' in the future and whether banks will be willing to supply it. The opening up of domestic markets and the rapid diffusion of financial innovations mean that risk sharing possibilities for firms are expanding, making heavy reliance on a single creditor less likely. As well, if firms undertake their own financial dealings in new market areas, the downside risks that their residual risk bearers will have to bear may be much higher than they used to be. Zai-tech operations are yielding large profits for many firms, but they can also lead to large losses, as the Tateho Chemical case showed. It is not just a case of firms opting out of paying insurance premiums to banks; banks, for their part, may become increasingly unwilling to insure the high risks that many corporate organisations are either facing (in their increasingly uncertain technological and production environments) or creating (through their forays into the world of financial engineering and wizardry).

Financial deregulation and liberalisation is also leading to a change in the informational apparatus of the capital market. The shift to greater 'securitisation' and the decreasing reliance on borrowings can be expected to lead to the development of competing information gathering agencies such as bond-rating agencies and credit rating agencies, and the growth of a

Table 4.5 Analysis of corporate interlocking among Sumitomo Bank and its top thirty shareholders[a]

Sumitomo's top 30 shareholders	Shareholding (per cent)	Sumitomo's shareholding in firm (per cent) (rank)	Sumitomo's share in firm's borrowings (per cent) (rank)
1 Sumitomo Mutual[b]	6.04	—	—
2 Nippon Mutual	4.48	—	—
3 Matsushita Electric[c]	3.61	4.65 (1)	—
4 Sumitomo Mining	2.84	3.88 (4)	12.54 (1)
5 Kubota	2.11	5.61 (3)	6.61 (4)
6 Nippon Steel	1.96	1.67 (6)	4.36 (4)
7 Daiichi Mutual	1.93	—	—
8 Kinto Spinning[d]	1.92	—	—
9 Sumitomo Trust & Banking	1.91	3.44 (8)	—
10 Sanyo Electric[c]	1.89	4.78 (2)	—
11 Sumitomo Marine & Fire Ins.	1.89	4.49 (2)	—
12 Kajima Corp.	1.89	4.93 (1)	18.73 (1)
13 Sumitomo Chemical	1.83	4.17 (3)	15.40 (1)
14 Sumitomo Corp.	1.77	4.75 (2)	11.54 (2)
15 Asahi Chemical	1.57	4.47 (2)	10.45 (1)

16	Takeda Chemical	1.28	4.61 (3)	37.50 (1)
17	Nippon Electric	1.21	5.11 (2)	16.15 (1)
18	Taiyo Mutual	1.19	—	—
19	Komatsu	1.15	4.84 (2)	20.63 (1)
20	Nippon Sheet Glass	1.11	5.34 (2)	21.03 (1)
21	Sumitomo Electric	1.05	3.29 (5)	18.80 (1)
22	Asahi Mutual	1.03	—	—
23	Hankyu Corp.	0.97	3.36 (2)	9.27 (3)
24	Nissan	0.81	3.02 (6)	7.28 (4)
25	C. Itoh	0.80	5.06 (2)	6.39 (3)
26	Kansai Electric	0.77	2.77 (4)	3.70 (5)
27	Shionogi	0.77	4.21 (3)	14.31 (1)
28	Long-Term Credit Bank	0.75	na	
29	Keihan Electric	0.63	4.78 (2)	11.95 (3)
30	Bridgestone Tire	0.63	3.28 (4)	8.38 (1)
Total		51.91		

Note: a The first two columns are as of March 1983; the second two as of March 1985.
b 'Mutual' in a company name is short for 'Mutual Life Insurance Co.'
c No bank borrowings.
d Non-listed company.

Sources: Shūkan tōyō keizai *Kigyō Keiretsu Sōran 1986 Nenban* Tokyo: Tōyō keizai shinpōsha, 1985; Sumitomo Bank *Sumitomo Ginkō '83* p. 31.

sophisticated securities analysis industry (Zaisei Kin'yū Jijō 1987). There have already been some developments in this direction, including the establishment of five bond-rating agencies since 1979 (Arai 1986; Kurosawa 1986).[15] But major developments may have to wait until there is thorough reform of the bond issuance system (Shōken Torihiki Shingikai 1986).

An important issue concerns the likely development of the takeover market in Japan (Business Tokyo 1987; Euromoney 1986). There is little evidence as yet that the role of main banks in intervening in problem firms is on the decline. Two recent cases where banks have required firms to undertake radical restructuring in return for financial assistance are the shipbuilders Hitachi Zosen and the Kurushima Dockyard (*Japan Economic Journal* 10 Jan 1987, p.17; 1 Nov 1986, p.14).

It is significant also that in the case of Tateho Chemical, a firm which has incurred losses from its zai-tech operations, Taiyo-Kobe Bank was reported to have sent in its officers to overhaul the firm's operations, in the typical pattern of main-bank intervention (*Japan Economic Journal* 3 Oct 1987, p.6).

It is highly likely that as long as the takeover market in Japan remains inactive the leading banks will continue to play this intervention role. But this is not to preclude the development of an American or Australian-style takeover market, independently of the main-bank system. There are various pressures at work—some domestic, others international—that suggest a gradual move towards the development of a more active external takeover market: the relative decline in the leverage of banks over firms, with the diversification of corporate finance and the rising proportion of firms that have no bank borrowings at all; the emergence of more firms with strong financial positions and active financial policies; the presence, with deregulation and the entry of foreign institutions, of many more players in the domestic market and greater fluidity in the relations between established domestic players; the fact that the gradual weakening in the 'lifetime' managerial employment system is lessening one of the underlying sources of corporate demand for stable shareholding arrangements (the protection of vulnerable 'permanent' management); the possibility that the weakening of the tradition of lifetime employment, particularly in the financial sector, will trigger a radical change in the attitudes of established domestic financial institutions to hostile takeovers; and the fact that Japanese firms are becoming increasingly active in foreign takeovers and acquisitions, and that international takeover bids into Japan are likely to increase in the future. It should not be overlooked either that, although 'serious' hostile bids are rare, there has been a history of share-cornering and green-mailing in Japan (Sheard 1986b: 19–20).

A big unknown in this equation is the stance that will be adopted by the regulatory authorities. In the past, the Ministry of Finance has facilitated the efforts of domestic players to internalise the takeover market, and at times has taken an interventionist stance itself—for instance, by using its administrative guidance over the securities companies and the stock exchanges to inhibit share-cornering activity (Sheard 1986b). It is likely that international takeovers of the kind that the Japanese firm Minebea faced (and successfully thwarted) in 1985 will become more common in the future.[16] With Japanese firms and banks becoming more active in their overseas acquisitions,[17] the Ministry of Finance will probably face increased pressure to take steps to remove the asymmetries between the access of foreign firms to the Japanese takeover market and that of Japanese firms in the United States and elsewhere, as takeovers in Japan develop into a serious market access issue.

Future scenarios

It is instructive to speculate on the future of the Japanese capital market, particularly in terms of the role of the main-bank system and the possible development of a takeover market, by sketching three possible scenarios.

Scenario one

The first scenario is a conservative one in terms of changes in the institutions that underlie the capital market at the microeconomic level. The monitoring role of main banks becomes somewhat less important as the proportion of borrowing-free firms increases and corporate bond markets become more developed; but main banks continue to substitute for bankruptcy or takeover by intervening in failing firms. Firms continue to develop more sophisticated financial management techniques and to expand their overseas acquisition strategies, but aggressive takeover strategies in the domestic market are still confined to a handful of maverick firms, which remain frustrated by the prevailing business ideology of opposition to hostile takeovers. This scenario is broadly consistent with the non-regulatory view of Japanese corporate organisation in the financial market.

Scenario two

In this scenario, the main-bank system becomes anachronistic as the Japanese capital market develops an impressive array of commercially oriented information-gathering agencies. The role of the banks in facilitating mergers, acquisitions and corporate reorganisations, once largely implicit in the main-bank system, is put on a much more commercial footing, with the larger banks upgrading their investment banking functions. Intercorporate shareholdings become much more fluid as firms extend their zai-tech operations to share dealing and aggressive takeover strategies in the domestic market. Listed Japanese firms increasingly become the targets of domestic and international takeover attempts.

Scenario three

In this scenario, the lifetime employment system in the financial markets breaks down and the major banks and securities companies switch to actively funding and advising on corporate takeover activity, including hostile domestic bids. The Ministry of Finance finds it increasingly difficult to block takeovers from overseas in the face of mounting international criticism of the asymmetry between Japan's takeover market and those of overseas countries.

The second and third scenarios are both more consistent with the regulatory view of the main-bank system and other corporate arrangements. The third scenario is perhaps more extreme, in that it not only implies that deregulation in the financial system will trigger changes in corporate behaviour, but it envisages feedback from these changes producing an acceleration of the process of financial deregulation itself.

This chapter has focused on the implications of continuing deregulation and developments in corporate finance for Japanese capital-market institutions at the microeconomic level, particularly the main-bank system, the takeover market and intercorporate shareholdings. It characterises the traditional capital market in Japan as one where informational activities such as the evaluation of, and intervention in, corporate management have taken place in an essentially 'non-market' setting as part of customer-type relationships and reciprocal and implicit business arrangements. It is argued that one consequence of the increasing liberalisation and shift towards 'securitisation' of Japan's financial markets could be the shifting of these informational services to a more overt market setting. Thus it is conceivable that, in time, agencies that collect and sell various kinds of corporate information could appropriate the informational role of the main-bank system, and that market-driven processes such as bankruptcy and takeovers could replace bank intervention as a way of effecting changes in corporate management and the allocation of corporate resources. A less radical outlook might be one where the element of specialised risk bearing in the main-bank system declines but the internalised takeover function of the system persists as long as the traditional stable shareholding arrangements continue.

PART II

Japan and the world economy

Japan now has a significant role in the world economy, especially in international currency and financial markets. One important reason for this is the domestic deregulation and liberalisation of capital flows discussed in part I (particularly chapter 2), which have made Japanese capital both available and attractive to the rest of the world.

Consequently, Japan must now take account of a range of international issues, and part II explores some of these. In chapter 5 Shinkai focuses on Japan as a supplier of capital and discusses whether Japan needs to run a current account surplus in order to be a supplier of capital; he also looks at the international impact of Japan's monetary and fiscal policies. In chapter 6 Fujii analyses the present role of the yen in the global economy and the effects of the internationalisation of the yen for Japan and the world. Finally, in chapter 7 Suzuki examines some issues that Japan must face if it is to become a world financial centre, and gives his views on the role the Japanese financial system should play in the world economy.

5 The global role of Japanese finance

Yoichi Shinkai

The global role of Japanese finance has been attracting considerable attention for the past few years. According to a recent IMF survey (1986: Table 19, p.96), in September 1985 the share of Japanese banks in the total international claims was larger than that of United States banks (25.8 per cent versus 23.4 per cent). The Japanese share in international bond issues has also increased significantly. The IMF survey shows (Table 35, p.110) that the share of international bond issues denominated in yen was 10.4 per cent in the first half of 1986. To quote Patrick (1987), 'since 1980 Japan has rather quietly but very quickly become an international financial superpower'.[1]

Japan's financial muscle is being felt in many parts of the world—for example, many financial transactions by Japanese institutions take place in Europe. But it is in Asian and Pacific countries that Japan's impact is likely to be strongest, since these are its largest trading partners and trade is the main channel through which Japanese capital is exported. Moreover, the shares of Asian countries in capital imports have been rising during the 1980s (IMF 1986: chart 4, p.7). Add the United States, whose huge imports of capital in recent years are well known, and the importance of the financial links between Japan and Asian–Pacific countries is immediately apparent.

This chapter attempts to assess some macroeconomic impacts of financial developments in Japan on the global economy. Attention is focused on the macroeconomic impacts because there are several important issues that must be discussed exclusively in a macroeconomic perspective; for example, the supply of Japanese capital to these countries and financial intermediation by Japan.

The first section briefly surveys the Japanese financial market, and the second section discusses the supply of capital by Japan. It argues that an economist's definition of capital exports is equivalent to surpluses in current account (roughly speaking, trade account), and that Japan is in a difficult situation because it is expected to simultaneously supply the world with capital and reduce its trade surplus. This leads to a discussion of Japan's role as a financial intermediary in the third section, which explores the possibility of

Japan's supplying long term capital without running large trade surpluses. The question of direct foreign investment in Asian–Pacific countries is also taken up there. The final section is concerned with the role of policies. Financial deregulation, and fiscal and monetary policies, should have some (perhaps considerable) effects on capital flows, interest rates and exchange rates, and theoretical and empirical studies of these topics are briefly summarised.

The Japanese financial market: an overview

The size of the Japanese financial market is remarkable. At the end of 1986, financial assets held by Japanese residents amounted to $11.8 trillion (Bank of Japan 1987); the corresponding figure for the United States at the end of 1984 was $13.0 trillion.[2] In Japan, bank loans outstanding stood at $3.4 trillion, and holdings of securities by financial institutions at $1.6 trillion (Bank of Japan 1987). These figures may be compared with the international claims of banks reporting to the Bank of International Settlements (BIS), which were $2.5 trillion in September 1985 (IMF 1986). The BIS reports on only the international positions of banks, but it covers nearly all the major banks in the world. Its data show that Japanese banks do business with their clients on a scale comparable with that on which the world's major banks do business with their foreign customers.

Japan's international assets and liabilities are fairly large. At the end of 1988, long term lending by Japanese residents stood at $179.2 billion and total holdings of foreign long term securities at $427.2 billion (Bank of Japan *Balance of Payments Monthly* April 1989, table 1.5). This is in addition to the short term financial claims held by Japanese residents of about $637 billion. On the liabilities side, foreigners held about $298 billion in Japanese securities, and Japanese resident banks had accumulated short term borrowings of more than $850 billion (this point will be discussed further in the third section).[3]

In 1988, Japanese corporations, households and the government together invested fewer funds than they raised domestically, and the balance ($80 billion) was invested abroad. So large an amount of funds could not have been invested abroad if international financial transactions had been tightly regulated. In fact, most Japanese foreign investments in 1988 took the form of net purchase of securities by Japanese residents, regulations on which are fairly liberal.[4] Other important instruments of foreign investment, namely direct investments and bank loans, are now completely deregulated (Shinkai 1988).

The supply of capital by Japan

As the Japanese financial market is large and mostly deregulated, Japan should be in a position to supply capital to those countries that need it.[5] This section discusses the possible role of Japan as a supplier of capital in the form

Table 5.1 Capital imports by Asian–Pacific countries

	Capital imports 1981–88[a]	% of 1987 GNP	Capital imports from Japan, 1982–88[b]
	$b		$b
North America	−793.4		−253.6
United States	−856.3	−18.9	−258.6
Canada	+62.9	+15.6	+5.0
Latin America	+55.2	+37.4	+7.2
Mexico	+49.9	+33.3	+4.6
Chile	+53	+33.3	+2.6
Oceania	−27.4	−14.5	+17.1
Australia	−27.4	0.0	+17.1
New Zealand	−0.0	−0.0	−0.0
Asia	+32		−73.1
China	−36.3	−12.1	−10.0
Taiwan	+73.7	na	−21.8
Hong Kong	−8.0	na	−43.3
Indonesia	+50.3	+76.2	+47.4
Korea	+7.0	+5.9	−24.2
Malaysia	+19.1	+64.0	+11.1
Philippines	−15.0	−43.9	+0.4
Singapore	−39.8	−193.9	−23.7
Thailand	−19.0	−40.8	−9.0
ASEAN (excl. Brunei)	−4.5		+26.2
Asian NICs[c]	+32.8		−113.1

Notes: a Sum total of trade balances. A negative number means capital imports; a positive number, exports.
   b Minus the sum total of Japanese trade balance with each region or country.
   c Taiwan, Korea, Hong Kong and Singapore.
Sources: IMF *International Financial Statistics Yearbook 1989*; IMF *Direction of Trade Statistics Yearbook 1989*.

of trade surpluses. Other forms of capital supply will be discussed in the next section.

The net capital outflow from a country is its excess of exports over imports.[6] The national income accounting identity states that net capital outflow equals the excess of national savings over domestic investment. Thus a capital-rich country does not invest all its savings domestically, but exports some of it to capital-poor countries. Foreign investments may take the form of direct investment, purchase of securities, or placing deposits in foreign banks. But they must equal the excess of exports over imports of goods and services.

Table 5.1 shows capital imports by Asian–Pacific countries in this form, overall and from Japan, for the past several years. Items are called 'capital imports', but they are actually cumulative values of trade imbalances.[7] The choice of countries and periods is somewhat arbitrary.

During the period from 1981 to 1988 total Japanese exports of capital amounted to about $370 billion, and table 5.1 shows that most Japanese capital exports went to the United States, which predominates not only in the last column of the table (with capital imports from Japan about four times as large as those of all Asian countries combined), but in the first column, overall capital imports. It is true that United States capital imports were not particularly large relative to GNP, but in absolute terms the United States was by far the largest capital importer (and is likely to remain so in the near future).

It may perhaps be of interest that some of the Asian–Pacific countries listed in table 5.1 were exporters of capital to Japan; notable examples are Australia, Indonesia and Malaysia. Since they are exporters of primary commodities to Japan, their trade surpluses with Japan are not surprising after all. Of the three countries, Australia was an overall importer of capital during the period; in other words, Australia imported a substantial (relative to GNP) amount of capital while running trade surpluses with Japan. In such a case it would be misleading to discuss the possible impacts of Japanese finance solely in terms of its trade balances with Asian–Pacific countries. This topic is taken up in the next section.

Japanese capital exports (excluding those to the United States) have not been very large. At $73 billion from 1982 to 1988, Japan's capital exports to other Asian countries may arguably be too small.[8]

In my view, capital exports from Japan are more likely to be depressed in the near future. Trade surpluses with the United States will be smaller than they have been in the past few years, thanks to the appreciation of the yen. Of the Asian countries that have imported Japanese capital, China, Korea and Singapore are trying to reduce their trade deficits with Japan. Japan has started 'restructuring' its economy at the request of the major economies of the West by stimulating domestic demand and further liberalising imports, thus reducing potentially large trade surpluses.[9] With capital importers trying to discourage Japan's capital exports, and with Japan trying to trim them down, it seems natural to expect that capital exports from Japan will fall.

Some Japanese economists hold the contrary view (for example, Onitsuka 1985, 1989). They invoke the theory of balance-of-payments stages to argue that Japan is now in the young-creditor stage,[10] where a country has a natural tendency to export capital. As a young creditor, Japan is rich in capital and tends to have an excess of savings over domestic investment, which should translate into a trade surplus. (This proposition ignores interest payments on debt, which are important for some countries.) The theory suggests that, whatever happens to exchange rates, capital exports from Japan will be maintained so long as its savings remain higher than its domestic investment. Whether the balance-of-payments stages view is correct or not, Japanese exports of capital are fairly large at present. Should Japan do more to reduce them, as the Venice Summit urged? Most Japanese capital has been exported by private institutions seeking higher returns than can be expected from domestic investments. They see nothing wrong with investing excess savings where the highest returns are expected. Moreover, this is one important way in which Japan can contribute to the economic development of capital-poor countries. And, while the United States is not capital-poor, it could be argued that without capital imports from Japan in the 1980s long term rates of interest in the United States would have been higher and industrial and housing investments smaller.[11]

But it is well known that all politicians, and a number of economists, argue that Japan should dramatically reduce its trade surplus—that is, its capital exports. Does Japan export too much capital? Even at its peak in 1987, Japan's trade surplus was only about 5 per cent of its GNP. In the latter half of the 19th century Britain exported capital at an average of 4 per cent of GNP, which suggests that on purely economic grounds Japanese capital exports in recent years have not been too large.[12] But political considerations carry more weight than purely economic reasoning. Capital exports from Japan in the sense discussed in this section are unwelcome everywhere.

Types of Japanese foreign investments

If Japan is to substantially reduce its trade surpluses with Asian–Pacific countries, those countries can no longer rely on Japan for net capital. They will have to find investment funds from other sources, either from their own savings or from, say, Europe. This does not imply, however, that the role of Japan as a provider of finance to these countries will cease to be important. For aside from being a net exporter of capital, Japan can invest abroad in various ways.

Japan's net international position (gross foreign assets minus gross foreign liabilities) at the end of 1988 was $292 billion, but its gross foreign assets (and liabilities) were much larger. Table 5.2 lists some important types of its foreign assets and liabilities. Gross assets at the end of 1986 stood at $1469 billion, most of which was held by private residents. Two large items are foreign securities and banks' short term assets. Direct investment and long term loans by financial institutions come next. These forms of investment (except for banks' short term assets) must have provided foreign corporations and governments with investment funds. They reflect, at least in part, Japan's past trade surpluses, but theoretically these types of investments could have been made without running a trade surplus. In that case Japan would have had larger international liabilities, perhaps in the form of short term instruments. Whether a 'borrow short and lend long' position is tenable will be discussed below.

The balance of long term loans is the result of past loans made each year. Table 5.2 records the balance held by Japanese residents, and there have been Euroyen loans as well in recent years. At the end of 1988 the balance of Euroyen loans to non-residents was $26 billion. Foreign loans have increased rapidly. In 1988 there were increases of 23 per cent and 28 per cent in loans by Japanese residents and Euroyen loans. Financial deregulation has no doubt played a crucial role in these developments. The value of official long term

Table 5.2　Japanese foreign assets and liabilities, 1986 and 1988

	1986	1988
	$b	$b
Assets	727.3	1,469.3
Private	632.6	1,266.9
direct investments	58.1	110.8
long term loans	69.2	123.7
securities	257.9	427.2
banks' short term assets	194.7	502.3
Official	94.7	202.4
international reserves	43.3	97.9
Liabilities	547.0	1,177.6
Private	494.0	1,119.3
securities	143.6	254.9
banks' short term liabilities	322.2	765.2
Official	52.9	58.2
securities	40.1	43.1
Net assets	180.4	291.7

Source:　Bank of Japan *Kokusai Shūshi Tōkei Geppō* (Balance of Payments Monthly) April 1989, Table 15.

loans was not small either; the balance at the end of 1986 was $20 billion, an increase of 43 per cent over the previous year (Ministry of Finance 1987).

No data are available on regional or country breakdowns of Japan's foreign loans. From newspaper reports and magazine articles it seems that the major portion is in the United States, and that a significant amount has been lent to heavily indebted less developed countries. Official loans are predominantly to Asian countries. Long term loans seem to contribute to economic development in borrowing countries, especially when loans are made by private agents to private borrowers. When such loans are negotiated, a lender carefully assesses the creditworthiness of a borrower and the profitability of a particular project. It is the profitable project by the well managed corporation that usually proves to be the sound investment. On the other hand, official loans or private loans to foreign governments sometimes go sour, which usually implies that the loans should not have been made in the first place.

Direct investment is even more conducive to economic development in host countries than private loans. Since the parent firm is directly involved, it will be very careful in assessing a project's profitability. Moreover, direct investment is accompanied by technology transfer, which increases productivity in host countries.

The balance of Japanese direct foreign investment was $110 billion in 1988 (see table 5.2). The upper panel of table 5.3 shows the regional breakdown of Japanese direct investment, where regional breakdowns are calculated as the cumulative values of past investments, and the lower panel compares Japanese investment with that of other countries. At the end of 1984 the Japanese

Table 5.3 Japanese direct investment

Investment in the Asian–Pacific area from 1951 to 1988

	$b	% of total
North America	75.1	40.3
Latin America[a]	1.9	1.0
Asia	32.2	17.3
Oceania	9.3	5.0
Total	186.4	100.0

Balances at year end 1988

		% of GNP[b]
Japan	110.8	3.8
US	326.9	6.7
UK	183.7	22.1
FRG	97.3	8.1
Holland	70.2	31.3
France	58.1	6.2
Canada	50.7	10.4

Note: a Chile and Mexico.
    b Calculated using GNP figures taken from IMF *International Financial Statistics*.
Source: JETRO *Sekai to Nihon no Kaigai Chokusetsu Tōshi* (Foreign Direct Investments by Japan and the World) 1990.

figure was small (relative to GNP), and the proportion at the end of 1988 was still under 4 per cent. Japan can certainly put more money into this form of foreign investment. However, since direct investments have long been deregulated, they will not increase appreciably because of the financial liberalisation of recent years.

The regional breakdowns perhaps give the impression that Oceania's share is a little too small. But relative to the GNPs of host countries Oceania's share is much larger, than, say, North America's. It must also be remembered that direct foreign investments are especially sensitive to host country regulations.

What is the industrial breakdown of Japanese direct investments? The source of the data in table 5.3 shows that the share of manufacturing was 26.7 per cent at the end of the 1988 fiscal year, with electrical machinery, metals, and items related to transportation chemicals heading the list. Of non-manufacturing investments, by far the largest shares were occupied by finance trade and mining. Though investment in real estate is being highly publicised these days, the data show that its share was only 11.4 per cent in 1988.

Holdings of securities are very large, on both the asset side and the liability side (see table 5.2). This means that outflows and inflows of funds in the form of security transactions have been large. In fact recent outflows of funds from Japan have been predominantly in this form. Table 5.4 shows that net purchases of securities (Japanese purchases minus purchases by foreigners) were roughly equal to total outflows.[13] The table also shows that financial institutions played the dominant role but that Japanese non-financial corporations were also active.

Table 5.4   Japanese financial transactions with non-residents

	1983	1984	1985	1986	1987	1988
	¥tr	¥tr	¥tr	¥tr	¥tr	¥tr
Outflow of funds	5.0	8.4	11.5	14.2	12.5	10.2
Net purchase of securities	0.4	6.0	10.0	16.5	12.7	7.1
Japanese purchase of foreign						
securities	3.8	7.4	14.1	17.1	12.9	11.2
(by corporations)	(1.6)	(3.6)	(7.6)	(5.8)	(5.1)	(3.2)
(by financial institutions)	(2.2)	(3.8)	(6.4)	(11.3)	(7.8)	(8.0)
Foreign purchase of Japanese						
securities	3.4	1.4	4.0	0.5	0.2	4.1

Source: Bank of Japan Chōsa Geppō June 1987.
Table updated for 1987 and 1989 using data contained in Bank of Japan Chōsa
Geppō June 1989, Table 14.

Investments in securities by private agents are commercially motivated, of
course; such investors are interested in expected yields and safety. In this
sense, security investments are almost exclusively directed towards advanced
countries. In fact most Japanese investments are in United States public and
private securities, though public bonds have been issued in Tokyo by less
developed countries from time to time. To the extent that security investments continue to dominate the market (this has been an important outcome of financial deregulation), Japan's contribution will be concentrated on
advanced countries. If Asian less developed countries are to be recipients of
larger Japanese investments, bank loans and bonds issued by international
organisations must be given active roles.

It has been noted that the primary commercial motivations are yields and
safety. Are securities issued by governments and corporations in an advanced
country safe? There is obviously a distinct probability of incurring large
exchange rate losses. Japanese life insurance companies, for example, invested
heavily in United States Treasury bonds, and because of the appreciation of
the dollar they had to write off more than $10 billion from their foreign assets
in 1986. Indeed, exchange risk is one of the most important considerations
that Japanese investors will have to take into account in the future. The share
of foreign assets in the portfolios of Japanese agents declined in 1986, probably because of the exchange risk consideration.

This section has dealt with long term Japanese investments abroad. It was
also noted at the outset that Japan can theoretically make these investments
without running trade surpluses. In other words, long term investments are
compatible with zero net exports of capital if a country incurs short term
debts of equal magnitudes. This lending long and borrowing short may be a
natural position for Japan to adopt as the world's banker, for one of the main
functions of a bank is to accept deposits (borrowing short) and make loans
(lending long)—that is, maturity transformation (Despres, Kindleberger and
Salant 1966).

At present the Japanese net international position is not zero, but table 5.2 indicates that Japan has been engaging in maturity transformation for some time. In 1988, Japanese resident banks had short term assets of $502 billion and short term liabilities of $765 billion—that is, their net short term position was minus $263 billion.[14] Since the short term public debt is small, private banks are the main borrowers of short term funds. The long term assets of Japan (not shown) were $833 billion, compared with long term debts of $312 billion—a net position of $521 billion. Thus Japan overall has been borrowing short and lending long. According to Ueno and associates this trend is likely to continue to the year 2005 (1987: tables 1–4, p.48).

Has the development just sketched nothing to do with the net asset position of Japan? Theoretically Japan's net position can be zero; but a country with a zero or negative net position is surely ill equipped to be a world banker. A bank always faces liquidity risks; that is, when the creditworthiness of a bank comes into question, there will be a run on its deposits. It is a private bank's capital that makes it creditworthy; in the case of a country the basis of trust must be its net asset position.[15] After all, Japan has had to experience quite a few trade surpluses in order to become a world banker.

The role of policy

This chapter has argued that the global role of Japanese finance is a result of financial liberalisation policy, and that United States–Japan bilateral developments in capital flows may reflect United States fiscal policy in the 1980s. This section focuses on the role of policy in changing the impact of Japanese finance on Asian–Pacific countries.

First, fiscal and monetary policies are discussed. In the period from 1982 to 1988 Japan's exports of capital to the United States amounted to $259 billion (see table 5.1). These flows were primarily in the form of long term security investments, and according to Frankel the main motive behind them was large return differentials (Frankel 1987). He also argues that the massive borrowing from abroad by the United States is the result of massive borrowing by the United States government. Many economists share his view. The loose fiscal and tight monetary policy in the United States, and (perhaps less importantly) the opposite policies in Japan, were responsible for the capital flows between the two countries.[16]

This implies that a change in United States macroeconomic policy will result in changes in net capital flows; but what will be the effects of Japanese policy changes? An Economic Planning Agency simulation exercise indicates that a fiscal expansion equal to 1 per cent of GNP brings about a $4 billion reduction in the trade surplus (EPA 1986b). In the case of policy coordination —that is, fiscal restraint by the United States and expansion by other countries—the Japanese trade balance will deteriorate by about $3 billion, the

United States balance will improve by about $15 billion, and Australia and Korea will see their balances (capital imports) deteriorate by about $1 billion and $0.1 billion respectively.[17] The results for Australia and Korea suggest that their trade balances are more strongly affected by United States policy than by Japanese policy.

The effects of a Japanese fiscal expansion on Oceania and the Asian newly industrialising countries are examined in a Ministry of Finance model (Takenaka et al. 1987). An increase in government expenditure equal to 1 per cent of GNP would bring about the following changes in trade balances: Japan, $6.4 billion; the United States, $1.7 billion; Oceania, $0.7 billion; and Asian newly industrialising countries, $0.3 billion. In the Ministry of Finance model, as in the Economic Planning Agency model, a fiscal expansion in Japan leads to little or no change in the yen exchange rate. This is in contrast to the case of a fiscal expansion in the United States, especially as analysed in United States models: a typical model explains the dollar appreciation up to 1985 almost exclusively in terms of the Reagan fiscal expansion program (Sachs and Roubini 1988). The United States models tend to predict that the yen will appreciate in response to a Japanese fiscal expansion, arguing that the liberalisation of Japan's financial markets will ensure that incipient capital inflows drive the yen upward. It is difficult to judge whether the Japanese or the United States models are better predictors.

The impacts of a fiscal expansion on trade balances and exchange rates will differ according to the particular set of assumptions employed by a model. It is no wonder that the editors of a recent conference volume have come to the conclusion that 'the clear lesson is that the real-financial linkages from fiscal policy are ambiguous' (Arndt and Richardson 1987: 38).

There is also some ambiguity about the effects of monetary policy. In the United States models, a monetary expansion tends to result in an exchange rate depreciation and a trade balance improvement; but a cut in the discount rate in Japan tends to result in a trade balance deterioration. Another interesting point emerges from a theoretical model that distinguishes short term and long term rates of interest (Fukao and Okubo 1984). In this model monetary restraint by the United States will depreciate the yen, which is not surprising; but it will also create inflows of short term funds to Japan and outflows of long term funds. If Japan can contribute financially to the rest of the world by borrowing short and lending long, as suggested earlier, this model highlights one way of encouraging its contribution.

Too much should not be expected of Japanese macroeconomic policies. First, their effects are uncertain in some cases, as already indicated.[18] Second, their effects are generally modest in size. Take the case of a Japanese fiscal expansion. A government purchase of (presumably domestic) goods and services amounting to 1 per cent of GNP is a fairly sweeping measure. At present it will be about ¥3 trillion—and remember, the much heralded package Japan prepared for the Venice Summit includes a government purchase of ¥5 trillion. The Economic Planning Agency and the Ministry of Finance models predict that that measure will reduce Japan's trade balance by $4 billion in the first case and $6 billion in the second. Compared with the current surplus of about $100 billion, these are small effects indeed. However, the effects in Oceania and the Asian newly industrialising countries may not be negligible. The Ministry of Finance model's predictions of $0.7 billion and $0.3 billion for their trade balance improvements are not negligible by comparison with the figures given in table 5.2. But whether trade balance improvements are truly welcome in these regions is another matter (see the second section of this chapter).

The Japanese package for the Venice Summit included a proposal to recycle $20 billion to the rest of the world; this was in addition to the $10 billion previously committed, which makes a total Japanese commitment of $30 billion over fiscal 1987–89. It is mostly contributions to the World Bank and other international organisations, and little of it will be aid grants to less developed countries (Ministry of Finance, A Background Briefing, 30 July 1987).

Of the $20 billion included in the Venice Summit proposal, the $9 billion earmarked as a contribution to the World Bank merits some comment. The contribution is supposed to be used by the Bank as development loans in cooperation with private financial institutions. Private institutions, and Japanese banks in particular, are reluctant to lend to less developed countries because of the default risks involved. Japanese banks operate on much smaller margins than United States banks (Nasu 1987), and they are understandably averse to risk.[19] But when loans are made in cooperation with the World Bank the risk of default is considerably reduced, and Japanese banks will be willing to lend a sum many times larger than $9 billion.

The Japanese financial market is large in size, and has now been effectively deregulated. Moreover, the Japanese economy now produces, and may continue to produce, a large excess of savings over domestic investments each year. With international financial transactions liberalised, Japanese excess savings are potentially a good source of finance for development projects in Asian–Pacific countries, and this is arguably the most important way Japan can contribute financially to the region. However, net capital exports from Japan are by definition equal to its trade (current account) surpluses, which seem to be unwelcome everywhere; and because of the hostility towards its trade surpluses, Japan must be reluctant to export net capital to countries that do not save enough to finance their investments.

Even without running large trade surpluses Japan can still serve as the world's financial intermediary, borrowing short and lending long; Japan is well equipped for this role. The Tokyo market handles large short term and long term transactions, and a variety of financial instruments are available. If a Japanese equivalent of the American treasury bill market open to non-financial agents were well established, Japan would be in a better position to be the world's financial centre. At present non-resident customers may find the Tokyo market a little inconvenient when they are investing short term yen funds. But Japan has been playing this intermediary role fairly extensively. Its short term debts are large, and are concentrated among banks, and its long term loans and bond underwritings (including Euroyen bonds) have been increasing rapidly.

Long term lending operations (bank loans and bond purchases) involve several risks—liquidity risk, exchange risk and default risk. Liquidity risk is concerned with a possible run on short term debts; that is, Japan may suddenly find it difficult to borrow short term in the world market. This risk will be much reduced if Japan's net international position is very positive, as it is now. Exchange risk is difficult to handle. It is not easy to hedge long term loans against exchange risk, and even if loans can be made in yen, borrowers have to bear the risk. Some method may perhaps be devised of softening the impact of exchange rate variations. At present, the risk of default by less developed countries is perhaps the most important factor in the sluggish flow of capital to these countries. Japan's policy-induced recycling proposals will help to reduce the risk of default.

As for the role of policy, financial liberalisation and recycling proposals have been mentioned earlier in this chapter. Fiscal and monetary policies may be expected to play a large role in promoting or depressing capital flows. Reagan's macroeconomic policy does seem to have produced huge capital flows from Japan to the United States. On the whole, however, Japanese macroeconomic policies will sometimes be ambiguous in their effects, and their effects will be small in size, according to several econometric and theoretical models.

6 The role of the yen in the Pacific and world economies

Makoto Fujii

During recent years the use of the yen in international transactions—the so-called 'internationalisation of the yen'—has progressed steadily, in step with the increasing weight of Japan in the world economy and the development of Japanese financial and capital markets.

Under these circumstances the internationalisation of the yen has been the focus of discussions both within Japan and in the world arena. There appears to be a genuine international consensus that the internationalisation of the yen is just as desirable as free trade or non-inflationary economic growth.

But the matter is more complex and obscure than it seems at first glance. Why is the internationalisation of the yen desirable? How can it realistically be achieved? What exactly is implied by the internationalisation of the yen? These apparently simple questions have not yet been answered. To clarify the point, I would like to quote at length a speech by Toyō Gyōten, Vice Minister of Finance of Japan, presented in New York in June 1986, in which he suggested two different ways of viewing the internationalisation of the yen. One way focused on the beneficial impacts of such a development and argued that:

> In order to facilitate the internationalisation of the yen, financial markets in Japan as well as in the Euroyen market need to be deregulated and fostered. Financial institutions both Japanese and non-Japanese, need to be given greater freedom of activity in these markets. Borrowers and investors need to have easier access to yen funds and yen instruments. In other words, this view places greater emphasis on the process of financial deregulation in Japan which becomes inevitably necessary in order to expedite the internationalisation of the yen. The process, rather than the goal, is the matter of the highest priority in this view. Most non-Japanese officials and private financiers seem to be advocates of this approach. (Gyōten 1987: 84)

Another approach to the issue, Gyōten suggested, is to:

... try to assess the impact of the internationalisation of the yen (ie, greater share for the yen in world trade and finance) on the functioning of the international monetary system and the respective role of the US and Japan in the world economy. For the last two decades, we have been discussing the so-called multi-reserve currency system, which would supposedly replace the present dollar-standard system. According to the advocates of such ideas, the yen and the German mark are expected to be used more widely in world trade and finance, so that they would share the burden of the key currency which is now borne by the dollar alone. Better distribution of the burden would enhance stability of the world monetary system.

There are, however, many unanswered questions. Is today's world ready, economically and politically, to accept such a transition? If a change is needed, what would be the desirable pattern of relationships among the US, Japan, and Europe? For Japan, particularly, the crucial question would be where to establish Japan's policy orientation vis-à-vis the US and Asia–Pacific region.

Financial deregulation in Japan is certainly an important process toward the goal of the internationalisation of the yen. It is a subject which deserves serious attention on an international level. (Gyōten 1987: 84–85)

But I believe, with Toyō Gyōten, that the time has now come to examine the internationalisation of the yen by focusing more on its implications for the world monetary system and foreign relationships.

This chapter first reviews the significance of the internationalisation of the yen by examining the effect of the internationalisation of the yen on the world and the Japanese economies, and the position of the yen and the dollar as international currencies. Then it presents data concerning the current situation with regard to the internationalisation of the yen on the global level. This discussion concentrates on the use of the yen in trade and financial transactions.

Finally, I give my own views on the prospects for the internationalisation of the yen and the approaches to doing so. The desirability of internationalising the yen and some of the conditions necessary for that internationalisation are also discussed.

The significance of internationalising the yen

Effects on the world economy

The internationalisation of the yen means that the currencies used in international transactions will be diversified. This introduces two considerations.

The first consideration is facilitating the control of exchange risks. Under the floating exchange rate regime, the tendency to rely on a single currency in international transactions involves exchange risks. There are many techniques—for example, futures options—that can reduce exchange risks. In addition, diversifying the currencies used in transactions spreads exchange risks, and thus it will help to promote international transactions.

The second consideration is the supplementation of the role of the dollar as the world's key currency. In the current international regime, the United States is responsible for stabilising the international monetary system by supplying dollars and maintaining the creditworthiness of the dollar as the instrument for clearing accounts in international transactions. From a policy standpoint, this imposes a greater responsibility on the United States than on other countries. But considering the decline in the relative importance of the United States economy since the 1960s, as the world economy has become increasingly pluralistic, there is a growing need to expand the currencies used to clear accounts in international transactions. Many economists believe that, in keeping with this trend, the internationalisation of the yen could supplement the role of the dollar and be a stabilising influence on the international monetary system.

Effect on the Japanese economy

It is self-evident that the internationalisation of the yen must affect Japan in various ways. It reduces the exchange risks for Japanese enterprises and banks, but at the same time it raises problems for Japan's economy.

In times of monetary restraint, the inflow of yen funds from the Euroyen market to Japan might hinder the effectiveness of domestic monetary policy. The rise in the yen assets held by non-residents might increase the exchange rate instability that arises from abrupt portfolio shifts between the yen and other currencies because of one-sided expectations about future exchange rate movements.

But there are, of course, more positive views. The effectiveness of Japan's domestic monetary policy can be sustained if the open-market operations of central banks make use of changes in interest rates. Violent fluctuations in exchange rates could be overcome through a macroeconomic stabilisation policy, and especially through policy coordination, as practised in the major industrialised countries.

In short, the internationalisation of the yen would require Japan to shoulder the responsibilities of being a key currency nation.

Issues related to the internationalisation of the yen

The position of the dollar as the international currency can be explained primarily by historical factors, but some other factors are also significant.

The first is the degree of international confidence in the country issuing the currency. The role of the dollar as the international currency ultimately boils down to a position where non-residents extend credit to the United

States. This amounts to an acknowledgment of the purchasing power of the United States, based on its capacity to generate financial services. Thus the role of the dollar as an international currency fundamentally rests on the stability of the United States economy and the confidence in it of foreign investors.

The second factor is the existence of free and diversified financial markets. Financial markets in the United States are conducive to a free and diversified use of funds: that is, there are few foreign exchange restrictions on the dollar; there are a number of large-scale, short term financial markets in bankers' acceptances, commercial paper and treasury bills available in the United States; non-residents can maintain their dollar assets through various easily convertible mechanisms; and the United States banking system has an extensive international network that is convenient for foreign payments.

This leads to a reconsideration of whether the conditions described above do indeed exist in Japan. In Japan, expanding economic activity has been achieved together with the stabilisation of prices. Japan's economic performance is fundamentally in good shape. The authorities are striving to maintain these conditions and to sustain confidence in the Japanese economy.

In principle, foreign exchange restrictions in Japan have been liberalised since 1980, and the Japanese banking system's international network has consequently been expanded. So the problem is whether Japan's financial and capital markets are flexible enough to cope with the needs of market participants.

The internationalisation of the yen: present situation

Trade transactions

The ratios of yen-denominated Japanese export and import transactions are both rising. In the fiscal year 1988, about 34 per cent of the total value of exports were denominated in yen, while the figure was 13 per cent for imports. In 1975, the corresponding figures were 17.5 per cent and 0.9 per cent respectively.[1] In West Germany, by comparison, over 80 per cent of exports and over 50 per cent of imports were denominated in Deutschmarks in 1987.

The ratio of yen-denominated transactions in terms of export categories is high for shipping (65.8 per cent in 1988), power generation equipment (41.7 per cent) and motors (37.7 per cent).[2] The ratio of yen-denominated transactions in imports is not high, because primary commodities constitute a large proportion of Japanese imports, and because it is the established practice to settle accounts for primary commodities such as petroleum in dollars.

What is the level of yen-denominated transactions as a ratio of all trade between Japan and its Asian–Pacific neighbours? On the basis of a regional breakdown of export transactions, in 1986 Southeast Asia stood at 39.0 per cent and Western Asia at 38.2 per cent; both were slightly above the overall

Table 6.1 Currency distribution of external medium term bank loans

	1985	1986	1987	1988	1989[a]
	%	%	%	%	%
US dollar	62.5	67.0	65.1	70.0	85.6
Yen	18.5	16.1	10.8	5.6	4.1
Sterling	3.4	6.4	14.7	14.1	1.7
Deutschmark	2.1	3.0	2.4	2.2	0.8
Swiss franc	3.0	2.1	0.7	0.3	0.2
ECU	7.1	2.2	2.4	2.8	3.9
Total[b]	48.3	53.1	87.1	118.5	140.0[c]

Notes: a The first quarter.
   b Billions of dollars.
   c At an annual rate.
Source: OECD *Financial Market Trends* May 1989.

average of 36.6 per cent. The comparable proportion for dollar-based transactions with Southeast Asia was 59.3 per cent, while the figure for Western
Asia was 38.2 per cent and the overall figure was 54.3 per cent. Exports to
Africa had the highest rate of yen denomination at 58.8 per cent, while
exports to the United States had the lowest—17.8 per cent.[3]

The economic relations between Japan and the Asian–Pacific region are
very close—about 30 per cent of Japan's total exports and imports are conducted within this region.[4] Furthermore, the percentage of the region's exports
and imports with Japan is high in comparison with its exports and imports
with other regions.

America's share of the Southeast Asian region's export and import trade is
also large. And many countries in this region export primary commodities,
transactions which are generally denominated in dollars. This reveals that the
dollar occupies a very important position in this region.

Thus, the close and extensive trade relations between Japan and the
countries of Southeast Asia are not in themselves sufficient to warrant a high
ratio of yen-denominated transactions.

Financial transactions

Yen-denominated bank loans are usually second only to dollar-denominated
bank loans (table 6.1). The proportion of outstanding foreign loans by
Japanese banks that are yen-denominated has been rising steadily in recent
years (table 6.2). In particular, there has been a rapid increase in Euroyen
loans by Japanese banks (table 6.3).

Recently this trend has been most conspicuous in medium and long term
yen-denominated loans by Japanese banks to Asia in the form of annual credit
commitments. The proportion of medium and long term yen-denominated

Table 6.2 Foreign loans by Japanese banks

	Outstanding ($b)		Share (%)	
	Foreign currencies	Yen	Foreign currencies	Yen
1980	54.9	9.1	85.8	14.2
1981	74.3	13.6	84.5	15.5
1982	92.5	15.5	85.6	14.4
1983	102.6	19.8	83.8	16.2
1984	123.0	29.0	80.9	19.1
1985	134.4	35.2	79.2	20.8
1986	169.1	57.2	74.7	25.3
1987	218.2	80.4	73.1	26.9
1988	275.5	99.7	73.4	26.6

Source: Ministry of Finance (Japan) *Kokusai Kin'yū Kyoku Nenpō* (Annual Report of the International Finance Bureau) (1989, Table 89).

Table 6.3 Euroyen loans by Japanese banks (billion yen)

	1983	1984	1985	1986	1987	1988
Loans to non-residents	192	468	1,399	2,385	3,253	3,321
Loans to residents	0	84	133	1,072	5,180	7,488

Note: Since 1985 loans to non-residents include medium and long term loans.
Source: Ministry of Finance (Japan) *Kokusai Kin'yū Kyoku Nenpō* (Annual Report of the International Finance Bureau) (1989, Table 90).

loans targeted at Asia rose from 13.6 per cent in 1984 to 16.7 per cent in 1988, and Asia is now second only to the OECD region as a recipient of these loans (table 6.4). This contrasts with the share of medium and long term dollar-denominated loans by Japanese banks to Asia, which remains constant at around 10 per cent.

Japanese banks began their drive to become a major source of loans for Asian countries in 1980. The relatively good economic performance that has characterised the region can be traced partly to the expanding role of loans by Japanese banks, and to the contributions of Hong Kong banks, which have long been successful creditors in Asia. The presence of Japanese funds has grown alongside the already considerable experience and expertise acquired through Japanese bank syndicate loans.

The flotation of international bonds (bonds issued by non-residents) is the area where the internationalisation of the yen is most clearly gaining ground. Originally, most flotations of yen-denominated bonds by non-residents took place in the Tokyo market, but since 1984 the regulations governing the issue of yen-denominated bonds in the Euromarket have gradually been relaxed.

Table 6.4 Medium and long term yen-denominated foreign loans, including Euroyen
(billion yen)

	1984	1985	1986	1987	1988	Percentage change from 1987 to 1988
International organisations	387	288	97	936	360	−66.3
OECD member countries	1,018	1,081	1,123	1,776	1,121	3.9
Eastern Europe	54	265	175	112	110	−34.0
Latin America	370	500	172	507	197	−65.6
Asia	293	623	593	697	368	−4.8
Middle East	1	5	—	5	1	—
Africa	32	131	121	87	39	−7.6
Others	2	3	1	10	5	−66.7
Total	2,156	2,896	2,281	4,130	2,201	−21.2

Source: Ministry of Finance (Japan) *Kokusai Kin'yū Kyoku Nenpō* (Annual Report of the
International Finance Bureau) (1987, 1989).

This is a factor in the remarkable increase in yen-denominated bond
flotations in Euromarkets (table 6.5): the share of yen-denominated bond
flotations in the total value of international bond flotations rose to 16 per cent
in 1987.

No country-by-country data are available for yen-denominated bond issues
in the Euromarket. But for those issued in the Tokyo market, the share of the
Asian–Pacific region was over 20 per cent (table 6.6).

However, in 1985, 1986 and 1987 the value of yen-denominated bond
flotations by foreign entities in the Euromarkets exceeded the value of
flotations in the Tokyo market (see table 6.5). One reason for this is that there
are many more regulations on flotations of yen-denominated bonds in the
Tokyo market than there are in the Euromarkets. This is a matter of considerable importance in the context of the further internationalisation of the yen.

Prospects for the internationalisation of the yen

Is the internationalisation of the yen desirable?

The internationalisation of the yen is desirable for the following reasons.
First, as noted earlier, the internationalisation of the yen will reduce exchange
risks by contributing to the diversification of the currencies used in
international transactions; second, as also noted earlier, internationalisation
will permit the yen to supplement the role of the dollar as the key currency
and reduce the burden on the United States as the key currency country; and
third, these effects will combine to make the international monetary system
more stable.

Table 6.5   International bond issues

	1983 ($m)	Share (%)	1984 ($m)	Share (%)	1985 ($m)	Share (%)	1986 ($m)	Share (%)	1987 ($m)	Share (%)
Euromarket issues	485	100	795	100	1,367	100	1,887	100	1,405	100
US dollar	384	79	636	80	978	72	1,191	63	581	41
Deutschmark	38	8	46	6	95	7	171	9	150	11
Yen	2	0	12	2	65	5	185	10	226	16
Sterling	19	4	40	5	58	4	106	6	151	11
ECU	20	4	30	4	70	5	71	4	74	5
Domestic market issues	278	100	280	100	310	100	394	100	403	100
US dollar	45	16	55	20	47	15	68	17	74	18
Swiss franc	143	51	126	45	150	48	232	59	243	60
Deutschmark	27	10	22	8	17	5	—	—	—	—
Yen	38	14	46	16	64	21	52	13	41	10
Sterling	8	3	12	4	10	3	4	1	—	—
Total	763	100	1,074	100	1,678	100	2,284	100	1,808	100
US dollar	430	56	691	64	1,024	61	1,259	55	655	36
Swiss franc	143	19	126	2	150	9	232	10	243	13
Deutschmark	65	9	68	6	112	7	171	7	150	8
Yen	40	5	58	5	129	8	237	10	266	15
Sterling	28	4	53	5	67	4	110	5	151	8
ECU	20	3	30	3	70	4	75	3	74	4

Sources: Morgan Guaranty Trust Company *World Financial Markets* June/July 1987; Ministry of Finance (Japan) *Kokusai Kin'yū Kyoku Nenpō* (Annual Report of the International Finance Bureau) (1989).

Table 6.6   Yen-denominated foreign bonds (samurai bonds) in the Tokyo market

	1981	1986	1987	1988	1970–88
	%	%	%	%	%
International institutions	35.9	36.9	40.2	46.4	33.7
Europe	39.2	27.4	21.6	27.9	30.5
North and South America	9.8	3.9	9.0	5.6	12.1
Asia & Oceania	15.1	28.5	27.7	14.6	22.1
Middle East & Africa	—	3.3	1.4	5.4	1.5
Total (billion yen)	612.5	785.0	497.5	797.2	8,948.1

Source: Ministry of Finance (Japan) *Kokusai Kin'yū Kyoku Nenpō* (Annual Report of the International Finance Bureau) (1987, 1989).

Of course, the issue at stake is not whether the internationalisation of the yen would be desirable for Japan alone; rather, the question should be whether internationalisation would be beneficial, at the same time, for all countries engaged in international transactions.

In order to stabilise the international monetary system under the floating exchange rate regime, it is especially desirable to have a strong currency besides the dollar to play a supplementary role. This need is increasing, which reflects the relative decline of the United States share in the world economy and its current tendency towards becoming a large accumulated debtor nation.

What should Japan do to bring about the internationalisation of the yen? The internationalisation of the yen requires Japan to shoulder the same responsibilities as the key currency country. Japan's economic performance must be good, and confidence in the yen must be maintained through a stringently disciplined economic policy. There is a need for financial and capital markets which give broad freedoms to both Japanese and non-Japanese institutions in fund raising and portfolio management.

It boils down to whether the yen will be regarded by market participants as an attractive currency to use in international transactions. In view of the importance of Japan in the world economy in the recent past, Japan must contribute to the world economy by trying to meet all these expectations. So the internationalisation of the yen is also desirable from this point of view.

Have the conditions for internationalisation been fulfilled?

Of the various efforts that Japan should make to achieve the internationalisation of the yen, economic performance has been high for some time now, and lately the correction of external imbalances has been making progress thanks to favourable domestic demand.

Next is the question of whether Japan has financial and capital markets which can easily be used for fund raising and portfolio management. Fund raising was discussed in the second section, but unfortunately there are no concrete data that would allow any statement about portfolio management. Some indication can be found in the share of the yen in the foreign currency reserves held by the monetary authorities of various countries. Table 6.7 shows that, although the share of the yen has been increasing of late, it is still trailing the dollar and the Deutschmark, and is low compared with the share occupied by issues of yen-denominated loans and bonds.

This seems to indicate that the need to hold yen reserves for foreign payments and exchange market intervention is not high, and at the same time that the yen is not yet attractive enough as a means of storing assets. More effort by the financial authorities is needed to facilitate short term market activity and make yen assets both profitable and easy to manage. Another stumbling block may be the remaining procedural restrictions on issues of yen-denominated bonds by non-residents in the Tokyo market.

Table 6.7 Shares of national currencies in total identified official foreign exchange reserves (per cent)

	1983	1984	1985	1986	1987	1988
US dollar	71.2	69.4	64.2	66.0	66.8	63.3
Deutschmark	11.6	12.3	14.9	14.9	14.7	16.2
Yen	4.9	5.6	7.8	7.6	7.1	7.2
Swiss franc	2.4	2.1	2.3	1.9	1.6	1.5

Note: The SDR value of ECUs issued against US dollars is added to the SDR value of
       US dollars, but the SDR value of ECUs issued against gold is excluded from the total.
Source: IMF *Annual Report 1989* Washington, DC.

In parallel with these readjustments in the financial environment, a positive response is expected from market participants who actually raise funds and manage portfolios. At the same time, a support structure must be provided by the governments concerned for the purpose of lending their active support to the stimulation of yen-based transactions. This would, of course, be based on a common realisation of the need to aim for a more stable international monetary system. To this end, the first priority is to secure the agreement of the various governments involved, beginning with the United States, about the value of such a framework. In this respect it should be emphasised that the cooperation and support of other governments are indispensable to the internationalisation of the yen, particularly the various governments in the Pacific area which have very close ties with Japan.

7 Japan's growing role as an international financial centre

Yoshio Suzuki

This chapter discusses the issues Japan must address in order to become a world financial centre, and sketches the role the Japanese financial system should play in the Pacific economy in the future.

Issues Japan must face to become a world financial centre

Financial reform in Japan seems likely to progress to the point where Japan will take on the role of a financial centre in the Pacific Basin. If this happens, the most important issue will be the stability of the resulting financial system within a framework of global markets.

The term 'stability of the financial system' has various meanings, but two are of primary importance in Japan. The first is stability in the sense of whether the new financial system in Japan, which will be constructed along lines that correspond to the realities of the Japanese economy, will in fact be consistent with financial systems in the rest of the world, thus making further change unnecessary. Consistency is particularly important for Japan today, as the Japanese economy constitutes one-tenth of the global economy, and Japan is the largest creditor in the world. The second meaning is stability in the sense of whether the new financial system will be able to perform the major functions of the old financial system, such as intermediation, risk avoidance and payments. Among these, the most important is the stability of the payments system, as pointed out in the Corrigan report (1987).

The internationalisation of regulations

Although the globalisation of financial markets has become possible because of the easing of regulations, there has also been an inverse effect. If domestic stability were overemphasised and all pressure towards change resisted, international stability would be sacrificed and, ironically, the system would become unstable.

A related issue is how to respond to the competition among systems that results from the competition among national markets. In a globalised situation both financial institutions and corporations may choose freely among systems and markets to make their transactions, so that when one country's regulations are less burdensome than another's, financial transactions will gravitate towards the former. In this process, markets in the less regulated countries will flourish, and those in the more regulated countries will decline. Various countries have changed their regulations in an effort to attract business for their financial institutions and financial markets; this motive was very strongly at work in the recent opening of offshore markets in various countries and in the 'Big Bang'[1] in London. In Japan as well, the Tokyo offshore market was established at the end of 1986, although in this case the development was more the result of demands from abroad.

Financial reform is therefore necessary from an international point of view. But there are many points of substance to consider. One of these is the ease with which systems in various countries might become overcompetitive. Precisely because the regulation and supervision of banks in offshore markets is less stringent than that in domestic markets, there is a need for caution about the consequences of such competition.

Another regulatory problem brought about by financial globalisation is the so-called 'level playing field' concept that has accompanied the intensification of competition among market participants. This concept calls not for changing a country's own system in order to make it as attractive as those in other countries, but rather demands that regulations in other countries be changed with the aim of offsetting the disadvantages of the home country's financial institutions or markets. For many years a principle has held among the major economies of national treatment in matters relating to the entry of foreign banks into a country and in the regulation of domestic activities (US Department of Treasury 1986).[2]

But, as globalisation has progressed and the competition among the world's financial institutions has become fiercer, trends antithetical to the spirit of this principle have emerged. One of these is the pressuring of other countries to ensure that they fulfil their promises of according national treatment. Another is the use of so-called reciprocity in financial activities. A third is the trend towards extra-territorial application of the regulations of a given home country to certain types of financial transactions.

The issue then becomes the standardisation of regulations across countries through multifaceted discussions and international agreements among the public authorities of the various countries. For example, in the summer of 1988 the Basel Committee on Banking Regulations and Supervisory Practices adopted an agreement on the international convergence of capital measurement and capital standards. It was then agreed that 45 per cent of hidden values, which arise as a result of long term holdings of equities valued in the balance sheet at the historic cost of acquisition, be counted as a capital element. It has been a practice of banks in Japan to cover losses not by reductions in capital but by liquidation of equities, and due consideration was given to this fact. The Japanese major banks are now expected to achieve the minimum standard for capital adequacy in the new framework without serious difficulties.

This 'level playing field' issue is also related to the differences among various national systems in the treatment of collateral requirements and the separation of types of business activities. If regulations are to be standardised, there will have to be a deepening of mutual understanding among countries of their financial systems so that the various players can compromise (Suzuki and Yomo 1986).

Ensuring the stability of the payments system

Financial reform has also brought major changes to the payments system, and one of the primary concerns is increased systemic risk among payment networks (Corrigan 1982, 1987; Stevens 1984). Systemic risk is now greater because of the various types of basic risk that have accompanied the liberalisation of finance—for example, interest rate risk (BIS 1986), liquidity risk, credit risk, and foreign exchange risk. In other words, the possibility has arisen of the insolvency of some participant in the payments system. The development of electronic funds transference and international payments systems has multiplied the quantities of funds being handled, and thus the possibility of an accident has inevitably increased (Vergari and Shue 1986). At a more fundamental level, there has been a shift in the method of payment from bank notes supplied by central banks to cheques, credit cards, and pre-authorised direct debits supplied by private financial institutions. The consequence has been a diminution of the 'finality' that bank notes used to bring to the payment system and an increase in the accumulation of arrears.

Several policies may be adopted to avoid systemic risk. For example, in the United States there is a cap policy.[3] Such a method of dealing with the problem cannot, however, go beyond certain limits. A more fundamental approach is to reduce arrears by recovering finality in payments. Bank notes, with all their finality, have been losing ground to payments mechanisms administered by the private sector because these mechanisms are more efficient. If, however, technological progress lowers the cost of settlement on a one-to-one basis, there will be no need to increase dependence on the private mechanisms to the point of ignoring the increased risks.

There are several payment mechanisms in use in the United States that have finality, and may indeed be called 'convenient electronic bank notes'— for example, the Fed wire.[4] In Japan as well there is a clear social need for such convenient electronic bank notes, and also a need for both the Bank of Japan and financial institutions in the private sector to meet this need. The BOJ Net, which is a counterpart of the Fed wire, started operation in the fall of 1988, and is also seeking to establish a system of delivery against payment for government securities.

The traditional notion of a safety net is also important in the effort to reduce the latent risks in the payments system. The ex ante safety net must, of course, be based on sound management, self-responsibility, and increased supervision and examination. In the ex post safety net, the central bank would form the nucleus as the lender of last resort; the net would also be supported by the deposit insurance system (Benston 1986; Kaufman 1986). It is necessary to remember, however, that too much reliance on ex post mechanisms will raise moral hazard and perhaps, ironically, lead to a reduction in the soundness of the system. To maintain orderly credit conditions, the ex ante elements of the framework must function properly and the ex post mechanisms must be adequate. Only in this fashion can the stability of the payments system be maintained through the complementary actions of both.

Tokyo's role as a financial centre

Based on the existing state of financial reforms, I would like to sketch my views on the future prospects of the Tokyo market, in particular its role as a financial centre.

The Tokyo market is now a top level world financial market in terms of the number of market participants, the number of transactions and the value of transactions (Goldenberg 1986). Tokyo, New York and London are the three biggest financial markets in the world. It could be argued that, with globalisation, the world financial market has already become polarised around these three centres. There are several reasons why the Tokyo market has developed so dramatically. One is its geographic position. Tokyo's location in time precisely midway between New York and London has allowed twenty-four-hour trading to take place. And since Japan's computer and telecommunications technology is extremely advanced, it has been easy to construct the infrastructure necessary for financial transactions. There is no doubt that these two factors, together with Japan's political stability and economic growth, propelled the Tokyo market into its extremely important position. Whether Japan can continue to take advantage of its geographic position and technological sophistication depends on whether it can overcome the problems noted earlier.

The supply of yen-denominated assets

If the Tokyo market does continue to be one of the three main financial markets, it can be expected to play the following roles in the world financial market.

First, it should supply stable and high quality yen-denominated financial assets; this is a natural role of a currency issuing country. To achieve this, it is necessary to promote an even higher degree of internationalisation and domestic financial liberalisation, to stimulate the development of financial instruments, and to institute a stable settlement system. However, this does not mean that Japan will merely supply yen assets to foreign investors as a vehicle for portfolio investment; Japan must realise that the yen will gradually become increasingly important in the international currency system.

What does this mean for the dollar? The dollar is overwhelmingly dominant in current international capital movements, and it will continue to be the key international currency, serving as a store of value, a measure of value and a settlement currency. However, it should be pointed out that the accumulation of external debt by the United States has been accelerating, while the exact opposite has been occurring in Japan. In 1987 the accumulated external debt of the United States reached $360 billion; on the other hand, the accumulated external assets of Japan amounted to $240 billion. The United States and Japan are now the largest debtor and creditor nations, respectively, in the world. This is not a transient phenomenon. It is estimated that in the 1990s the figures for the United States and Japan will balloon to the trillion dollar level—positive for Japan, negative for the United States.

If the United States continues to accumulate debt while the dollar maintains its status as the key currency, what will happen? It will be like a rowboat ferrying an elephant: the slightest trouble in the American economy, which will be preoccupied with debt management, will make the international currency system pitch and roll because of the wide acceptance of the key international currency. On the other hand, if the largest creditor nation does not open up its domestic market and allow its financial and capital markets and its currency to be used as international public goods, then, as history teaches, the struggle for power between the old and the new will become violent; economic blocs will form, trade frictions will worsen, and finally world depression or war will break out. If the conditions in which Japan is temporarily the world's largest creditor nation continue over a long period, the yen should take the role of an international currency. In that case, should Japan aim for the establishment of an international currency system in which the yen is the one and only key currency? The answer is clearly no!

In the 21st century, no single country will be able to exercise hegemony— as mirrored in the expressions Pax Britannica and Pax Americana—in the economic, military and political spheres. Rather, the world will be characterised by a system of multipolar international cooperation. In that system Japan no doubt will actively supply international public goods. Accordingly, a realistic international currency system will be a system of multiple key currencies in which the dollar, the yen and the European currency unit (ECU) coexist. In that case, whether the yen should fill a major independent role or should be the leading player in an ECU-style Pacific area currency (PACU, to coin a word) is a question that requires careful study.

Coordination of world money flows

The second role for the Tokyo financial market while ever Japan remains among the world leaders is to function as the place where the world's money flows are coordinated. The circulation of funds from surplus-capital countries to deficit-capital countries and the recycling of excess savings from a country to the rest of the world is certainly a task for international markets. This role is most efficiently performed in offshore markets, where transactions are entirely unregulated. When OPEC funds were being recycled, for instance, it was exclusively offshore markets in London and other places that were employed to do this.

In December 1986 the Tokyo offshore market, which handles offshore transactions of the same type as America's International Banking Facility, was founded. The balance of funds in the Tokyo offshore market in December 1988 was around $410 billion, a scale which almost equals that of the Hong Kong market and exceeds that of the Singapore market. However, in Tokyo this recycling function should be performed not only by the offshore market but also by the domestic market. This is because, since Japan is the world's biggest creditor, it should consider recycling directly. When OPEC was amassing huge sums of oil money, the creditors and debtors were the developing countries; therefore the role played by the financial intermediaries of the developed countries was indispensable. Basically, OPEC deposited funds in the Euromarket and the less developed non-oil countries received Euro syndicate loans. Now, however, the situation has completely changed: the biggest creditor nation is Japan, the biggest debtor nation is the United States, and so the coordination of the flow of funds among developed nations will not necessarily involve intermediation. Japan, which can accurately assess the creditworthiness of borrowing nations, might invest in assets that have particularly high risk relative to that of deposits, and borrowing countries might diversify their loans through the issue of bonds and commercial paper.

With recycling, the investments that will from now on require examination are those going to the developing countries. In my view Japan should circulate its accumulated external assets to these countries, but as a practical matter Japan is facing the accumulated debt problem, so it is quite a difficult decision to recycle national assets to high-risk developing countries whose capacity to repay is in doubt. But the goal can be realised through the following steps: providing funds to further international cooperation under the aegis of such entities as the World Bank; giving priority to supplying credit to projects that will expand productive capacity; and systematically combining public financing and foreign aid from the Japanese government.

The core of Pacific Basin financial markets

The third role of the Tokyo market is to function as the core of Pacific Basin financial markets. There are various aspects of this role. One of these is what is called the complementarity of markets. Already the Sydney futures market and New York's COMEX (Commodity Exchange, Inc.) in one instance, and the offshore markets of Montreal, Amsterdam and Vancouver in another, have concluded contracts on mutual settlement: the unification of markets is proceeding and, learning from this, the Tokyo market believes that it should promote complementarity by cooperating with all Pacific Basin financial markets.

These neighbouring markets have the smallest time difference risks. Gains from complementarity, if matters are left to the market mechanism, occur to the extent that there are markets nearby. In this connection it should be noted that when the Tokyo offshore market was established, the offshore markets of Hong Kong and Singapore each experienced an increase of nearly 15 per cent in their volume of transactions; and if cooperation grows, even greater increases in market volumes can be expected.

Another point is the transformation of the Tokyo market into a department store that deals in the financial products of the world and provides these services to Pacific Basin investors. For instance, a very important market in American government bonds has already been formed in Tokyo. Its daily volume of transactions is $2-3 billion—not all that large, but there are many occasions when it leads the New York market on pricing. There are further examples, such as the futures market, of trading in foreign financial products in Tokyo, and the time may come when all the financial instruments—government bonds, certificates of deposit, commercial papers, and so on—of the principal developed countries will be able to be bought and sold in Tokyo. If this comes to pass, domestic and foreign investors will gain from being able to choose from a wide range of investment vehicles.

Tokyo as an information gathering centre

The fourth role of the Tokyo market is to bring into full play its capacity as an information gathering centre. Since information is indispensable for financial transactions, the degree of profitability and the capacity to control risk depend on the power to gather information. It is clear that the financial service industry specialises in the know-how of risk management and profits through information processing. Such information can be obtained cheaply at any time anywhere because of the development of computer and communications technology.

In order to get information in Sydney on the New York exchange rate market and stock market, it is not necessary to have a representative in New York. Pushing one terminal key in Sydney supplies all the New York information necessary. Perhaps this should be called 'low-grade' information. In contrast, there is also what should be called 'upper grade' or 'emotional' information—information transmitted after meeting someone face to face, for example, information related to future events, confidential information, and tangential information.

Because low-grade information has become readily accessible due to progress in information processing, upper grade information has become extremely expensive. Hence the phenomenon called 'high tech, high touch', which has brought financial institutions thronging to the City in London and to Wall Street in New York. In Tokyo too there is an area of about one and a half square kilometers called the 'Tokyo triangle', where about 80 per cent of financial institutions are concentrated. This information function of the Tokyo financial market is important, since it can be used relatively inexpensively in the Pacific Basin.

PART III

Pacific financial markets

Part III explores some specific national perspectives on the significance of the changes in Japan's financial policies. Broadly, it deals with the meaning of those changes for some Pacific economies: Hong Kong and Singapore; New Zealand; and Australia. In chapter 8 Ong deals with the impact of Japan's financial deregulation, including the introduction of the Tokyo offshore market, on the Hong Kong and Singapore markets; his discussion complements Suzuki's treatment in chapter 7 of the role of Tokyo as a financial centre. In chapter 9 Nicholl and Brady examine the role of the yen, and the factors influencing its use, in New Zealand's international trade and financial transactions, providing an interesting contrast to the general discussion in chapter 6 of the use of the yen in the international financial system. In chapter 10 Higgins discusses the policy responses of a small, open economy like Australia to the financial deregulation described in chapter 2 and to the international coordination of economic policy.

8 The impact of Japan's financial deregulation on Singapore and Hong Kong

Ong Nai Pew

In the 1980s Japan's net long term capital outflows have been funded by a high personal savings rate, and have persistently exceeded the current account surplus. Japan's net excess domestic savings can be expected to fall as a share of GNP in the future. Sizeable long term capital outflows will continue, however, with a larger share being funded by investment income from abroad. In the Asian–Pacific region, China, Australasia and ASEAN (except Singapore) will continue to be important capital-deficit areas for some time to come. Taiwan, Hong Kong, Singapore and South Korea can be expected to join Japan as important sources of capital.

From 1981 to 1988, total long term capital outflows from Japan surged from $9.7 billion to over $130 billion,[1] with savers continuing to pour their capital into mutual, trust, pension, and insurance funds.[2] These savings are increasingly invested overseas, and have funded the Eurodollar and Asian dollar markets and, more recently, the Euroyen and the fledgling Asian yen markets.[3]

Since 1981 Japanese financial and non-financial corporations have followed these savings flows abroad and established a network of branches and subsidiaries in the financial centres of America, Europe, and Asia. The total assets of Japan's banking system now stand on a par with the total assets of United States commercial banks. Internationally, Japanese banks have become the world's largest creditors; they now account for a third of international bank assets (far ahead of United States banks),[4] and have become a potent force in determining where international financial business is transacted. Japanese corporations are estimated to have relied on overseas borrowings for up to a quarter of their external funding in 1985 and 1986. These corporations have raised funds in the Euromarkets and Asian offshore markets (often at better rates than banks could command) and used them to purchase financial assets domestically or abroad.

All this has spurred the Japanese Ministry of Finance to deregulate the domestic capital and money markets in order to bring business back to Tokyo. This is evident in Japan's fairly successful policies to promote non-resident shogun and samurai bonds, loans to non-residents, the Tokyo offshore market and the futures markets. All the big international financial institutions are now attracted to Tokyo, despite its high costs and taxes.

The analytical framework

An offshore financial centre can be defined as a place where international financial institutions channel funds raised globally to meet global market demands in an environment relatively free of financial regulation. Offshore financial activities are now divided into three time zones, and most offshore and international financial activities are readily substitutable between competing centres within each time zone. Tokyo is increasingly the dominant centre in the Asian–Pacific time zone, and both Hong Kong and Singapore still transact more than strictly regional business, and have strong links with London and New York.

The process of deregulation in Japan has produced two effects. First, it has meant the release of Japanese savings on to the world market, which has inevitably attracted international fund raising activity to the Asian–Pacific time zone, increasingly at the expense of the western hemisphere. Another factor in this shift is the phenomenal rise of Japanese securities houses and banks, which also retain the dominant position in Hong Kong (and, arguably, in Singapore).

Second, this rise in the volume of Asian–Pacific offshore financing is accompanied by its concentration in Tokyo, partly at the expense of Hong Kong and Singapore, a phenomenon exemplified by the establishment of the Tokyo offshore market. Associated with this is the rise in popularity of yen-based instruments, which are not as heavily used in the other Asian financial centres. A further boost to the rise in Tokyo's market share in the Asian–Pacific region is the institutionalisation of round-the-clock global trading in international securities, with New York, London, and Tokyo forming the international nodes, as is evident in the recent concentration of the largest American and European securities houses and banks on Tokyo. This has diverted the internal resources of these corporations to Tokyo, as well as scarce financial professionals, at the expense of Singapore and Hong Kong. This concentration is accentuated by Japanese Ministry of Finance measures to attract some financial business from the Euromarkets and New York, especially foreign exchange transactions, foreign bond issues, foreign syndicated and project loans, and trading in foreign and Japanese securities.

The competition for market shares in the Asian–Pacific time zone continues. Since offshore financing activities are carried out primarily by international financial institutions, the impact of Japan's deregulation is analysed here in terms of its effect on the location decisions of these institutions. The main determinants of this are: the sizes of domestic and neighbouring markets, and the concentration of market players; taxes and costs; and regulations and environment. These are the important factors to be taken into account in explaining the impact of Japan's financial deregulation on Singapore and Hong Kong.

International banking

The rise of Japan as the dominant source of international credit will continue to increase the interbank flow of funds within the Asian–Pacific region, despite the global trend towards securitisation.

In general, the Asian–Pacific credit market is still primarily an Asian dollar market, though yen-denominated loans have increased considerably. Apart from well recognised subsidiaries of Japanese companies, prominent regional borrowers have come from Australia, South Korea, New Zealand, China, India, Hong Kong and the ASEAN bloc. Japanese banks prefer to book syndicated loans abroad in order to avoid paying tax. Thus the increase in foreign loans from Tokyo before the Tokyo offshore market opened was accompanied by a marked strengthening of Japanese banks in Hong Kong and Singapore, owing to their larger sources of funds and better connections with Japanese corporations in the region. With higher Japanese direct investments expected in the region, Japanese banks would be advantageously placed to lend to Japanese corporations in the region, or to guarantee or underwrite their loans. Not surprisingly, Japanese banks have succeeded in capturing a significant share of the Asian–Pacific loan market since 1984. While Hong Kong has reaped most of the benefit from this, the number of Japanese financial institutions in Singapore has also grown. Recent Japanese deregulation also precipitated a sharp rise in Euroyen loans, primarily by overseas subsidiaries and branches of Japanese banks—loans that have eaten into Eurodollar and Asian dollar credit markets.[5]

The Tokyo offshore market

The Tokyo offshore market, which opened on 19 December 1986, is characterised by the following features: offshore accounts are not subject to withholding tax but still incur stamp duties and municipal taxes; offshore banking income still faces the corporate tax rate of about 48 per cent; transactions in securities are prohibited; and offshore and domestic markets are strictly separated, which requires financial institutions to square their accounts at the end of every day. Only non-residents and overseas subsidiaries can deposit and borrow in the offshore market. The market provides international banking connections for Japanese regional banks and other smaller banks that do not have overseas branches. Some liberalisation of the market's operating conditions is likely in the next few years, especially if the market is seen to be faltering.

A cursory examination might suggest that the Tokyo offshore market could pose a serious threat to both Singapore and Hong Kong, the leading offshore banking centres in the Asian–Pacific region. First, some interbank and forex business with centres in the region or other international off-time zones could shift to Tokyo as it assumes its role as the main international centre in the Asian–Pacific region. A corporation operating in the Tokyo market and another market in the Asian–Pacific time zone wishing to justify within the corporation the high cost of running its Tokyo offices could transfer its money and foreign exchange business in the time zone from Singapore or Hong Kong to Tokyo. Second, the new concentration of international banks in Tokyo has brought together market intelligence and contacts which could enable Tokyo-based banks to penetrate regional markets as well. The main thrust would probably be towards the North Asian bloc. Sovereign and well known corporate borrowers could also be attracted by the vast funds available in Tokyo. To weigh these arguments requires a detailed assessment of the recent experience of the offshore banking markets of Singapore and Hong Kong.

The offshore markets of Singapore and Hong Kong

Singapore's offshore Asian Currency Unit market and Hong Kong's foreign currency market are the two largest money markets in the Asian–Pacific region, each with well over $200 billion in assets by the end of 1986. In size they rank equal third behind London and New York. The new Tokyo offshore market has grown to about $134 billion in assets in its first quarter of business, without diminishing the sizes of the Hong Kong and Singapore markets.

Offshore business in Singapore is taxed at a concessionary 10 per cent rate. Securities transactions are permitted, and the costs of personnel and premises are about a third of those in Tokyo. Only a fifth of the Asian Currency Unit activity in Singapore consists of loans to and deposits by non-bank entities; the remaining four-fifths are interbank activities. Offshore syndicated loans benefit from a tax holiday, and onshore loans up to S$30 million are permitted. The structure of Hong Kong's foreign currency market is remarkably similar to that of Singapore's offshore market. Although the absolute number of banks and deposit-taking companies (DTCs) in Hong Kong declined from 489 in 1982 to 440 in 1986, their offshore assets increased from $83.9 billion to $211.7 billion. The rise in non-bank deposits was fuelled by the abolition of withholding tax on deposits by non-residents. A low corporate tax rate of 18 per cent is applied to all international banks and DTCs. Unlike the Tokyo offshore market, offshore banks in Hong Kong (including DTCs) and Singapore are allowed to undertake securities-related business, including investment management.

The principal interbank markets for Singapore are north Asia, Western Europe and ASEAN. Between 1985 and 1987, more than a third of Singapore's interbank business has been transacted with regions outside the Asian–Pacific zone. Hong Kong's interbank market distribution is similar to

Singapore's, except that it has stronger ties with Western Europe than with ASEAN. In both centres, interbank dealings with Japan expanded considerably between 1982 and 1986, while dealings with the United Kingdom have declined in relative importance.

For non-bank loans, Singapore's main markets are north Asia, Australasia and ASEAN, these three regions accounting for about three-quarters of all non-bank loans. About a fifth of all non-bank loans are transacted with regions outside the Asian–Pacific time zone. Hong Kong's markets are mainly north Asia, ASEAN and the Caribbean (re-routed back to the Asian–Pacific region). Hong Kong is still the favoured booking centre in the region but it has lost some of its loan syndication to Singapore, and it has lost more as a result of global securitisation. Banks in the Tokyo offshore market have also made a few syndicated loans to traditional clients of Singapore and Hong Kong. Large-scale international borrowers of syndicated and project funds in the Asian–Pacific region, especially sovereign states and supra-national organisations, are attracted by Tokyo's newly deregulated onshore credit market as well, given the availability of yen and dollar funds with long maturities.

The main sources of non-bank deposits for Singapore are north Asia, Western Europe and ASEAN. The steep rise in non-bank deposits in Hong Kong is partly accounted for by funds from Japan, Taiwan and Indonesia. Non-bank depositors (including foreign state agencies and banks seeking lower country risk) can now turn to Tokyo as well as Singapore. Japanese subsidiaries in Southeast Asia may also be induced to deposit directly in the Tokyo offshore market. However, early indications are that losses by Hong Kong and Singapore to Tokyo of non-bank deposits are not too substantial. Compensating for this is the increase in the booking of non-bank loans in the two centres.

A recent development is the rise of offshore yen funding business with the establishment of the Tokyo offshore market. This is currently a preserve of Japanese financial institutions. Since there are many Japanese merchant banks and finance houses in Hong Kong, it has captured some of the yen-based credit market.

In recent years, differentials in regional growth rates have favoured Singapore in interbank activities, but not so much in non-bank activities. For interbank activities, the contributions of the faster growth of transactions with Japan, Taiwan, Australasia, and Western Europe exceeded the effect of slower growth in other regions. From 1982 to 1986 offshore activities with ASEAN, South Korea, China, Latin America and the Middle East grew more slowly than those with other markets.

Both Hong Kong and Singapore are expected to retain their positions as leading offshore banking centres in the Asian–Pacific time zone, unless further deregulation takes place in the Tokyo offshore market. The resilience of these centres in the face of Japan's financial deregulation can be attributed to three factors.

First, the proximity and familiarity of bankers in these centres with their hinterland—broadly, the Asian–Pacific rim from South Korea through ASEAN, to India in the west and Australia in the east—makes penetration by Tokyo-based institutions uneconomic. While bankers from Hong Kong and Singapore compete for privileged ties with non-bank borrowers and depositors in this region, their Tokyo-based counterparts are simply too far away. The only important exception might be the business offered by large, well known borrowers (and depositors) from this hinterland, such as government and state agencies, that could bargain for fine rates from loan-hungry Tokyo-based banks. The comparative advantage for Singapore and Hong Kong banks lies in assessing and lending to regional companies and state-run enterprises which have not achieved adequate recognition and credit ranking in Tokyo.

Second, compounding the advantage of proximity to this hinterland, both centres have had a significant head start in attracting international banks and other financial institutions with established networks of contacts throughout the region, so that much regional interbank business is transacted within each centre. The concentration of European and American financial houses in both centres has been reinforced recently by the arrival of well financed subsidiaries and branches of Japanese financial institutions. Additionally, the long established global linkages offered by Hong Kong and Singapore make it useful for Japanese financial institutions to direct sizeable amounts of their business with clients in the European and American time zones through branches or correspondent offices in these two centres. Thus about half the interbank claims in the Tokyo offshore market were accounted for by Singapore and Hong Kong. Dealings by Japanese banks with their overseas branches amounted to slightly more than 70 per cent of all transactions in the Tokyo offshore market, most being conducted between Tokyo and Hong Kong, Singapore and Europe. Unless there is a relaxation of the prohibition against using domestic funds in the Tokyo offshore market, there will be no clear cost-of-funds advantage to funding and making loans in that market as opposed to Hong Kong and Singapore.

Third, this advantage in interbank operations is enhanced by the cost-effective, friendly, low-tax regulatory environment for offshore financial institutions. The ready supply of young professionals in Singapore and Hong Kong who are proficient in English puts an effective ceiling on the salaries of middle-level financial managers, which keeps the cost of overheads down. This advantage has diminished in the case of Hong Kong, however, as 1997 approaches. According to some bankers, the basic costs associated with banking and fund management (office rent, clerical help, telecommunications charges and so on) in Hong Kong are on average a third of those in Tokyo. They are even lower in Singapore.[6] Auxiliary services (in English), especially international legal and accounting assistance, are more readily available and cost-effective in both Hong Kong and Singapore than they are in Tokyo.

While the Hong Kong market is more deregulated than Singapore's, this has exacted a high price in the form of occasional, sometimes spectacular, bank failures. Hong Kong also has a reputation as a tax haven. The advantages of double-taxation arrangements are thus open to Singapore but not to Hong Kong for offshore depositors. If Japan's plan to impose its high domestic tax rate on Japanese subsidiaries (deposit-taking companies) in Hong Kong because of the latter's status as a tax haven goes through, and the proposed higher capital-to-asset ratios are imposed on deposit-taking companies, Hong Kong could lose its advantage as Asia's booking centre for offshore loans.

Forex operations

The surge of yen–dollar transactions of the past few years owed more to the liberalisation of Japan's capital markets following the Yen–Dollar Accord of 1984 than to the increase in trade transactions.[7] The Japanese Ministry of Finance has pursued the objective of internationalising the yen by encouraging fund raising through the Euroyen and yen-based foreign bond and credit markets. Up to 85 per cent of these involve swaps with the US dollar and other currencies. Huge purchases of foreign securities by Japanese institutions, especially trust funds and insurance companies, have also encouraged hedging activities through swaps and other techniques. There have been steady increases in foreign investments and trading in Japanese securities since 1980.[8] Tokyo has thus become the undisputed centre for spot and swap transactions in the Asian–Pacific zone. Tokyo's forex traders have also developed expertise in trading in Deutschmarks and Swiss francs, and can now compete for this market segment with Singapore. Daily foreign exchange turnover in Tokyo averages over $50 billion, compared with $58 billion for New York and $90 billion for London.

The Tokyo foreign exchange market's virtual tenfold expansion from 1981 to 1986 has taken away a finite market share (especially in yen–dollar transactions) in the Asian–Pacific region. However, after an initial market-grabbing phase, the overall expansion of forex transactions following Tokyo's deregulation has benefited Singapore and Hong Kong. Singapore has already established its position as the largest forex centre (over $35 billion) in Asia after Tokyo, and foreign exchange banks have significant depth and experience as well as excellent facilities. Hong Kong is estimated to have grown almost as fast as Singapore. Thus, while the increase in forex operations in Japan has been spectacular over the past seven years, this has not deprived Singapore and Hong Kong of opportunities for growth. Some reasons can be adduced for this.

First, the expanding demand for forex operations originating in Japan has been accompanied by a worldwide increase in forex transactions with the extremely volatile currency fluctuations in the 1980s. Thus there is a lot of room for established forex centres to grow.

Second, forex operations are transactions between financial institutions that are readily substitutable between countries. The concentration of international financial institutions in Hong Kong and Singapore (including subsidiaries of Japanese securities houses that cannot transact forex trade in Japan) means that they have natural bases that cannot easily be bid away by the newly emerging Tokyo market. This advantage is reinforced by the cost-effectiveness of both centres relative to Tokyo. It is estimated that the unit cost of forex operations in Hong Kong is about a quarter of that in Tokyo, and even less in Singapore. There is also a good supply of traders in these centres, especially Singapore. These cost advantages have not been offset by the economies of scale of the larger unit orders in Tokyo. The cost-effectiveness of both centres has enabled them to feed off the market for forex transactions in Japan.

Third, forex trading requires liquidity. Singapore and Hong Kong are the second and third legs to Tokyo, and Singapore occupies the tail-end of the Asian–Pacific trading time zone. Thus the rise of forex trading in Japan and in yen means added business for Singapore, especially if it extends its trading hours to match Sydney on the one side and to link with New York on the other.

The offshore bond market

Japan's domestic bond market now ranks as the second largest in the world. The most spectacular growth, however, has been in Japan's purchases of offshore Eurocurrency bonds since 1982, which account for close to half of total international bond issues in the Euromarket. Partly in response to deregulation and in an effort to steer some of this business back to Tokyo, the Ministry of Finance reopened the shogun bond market. With the liberalising measures implemented in 1984, samurai bond issues for non-residents also grew. These onshore foreign bond markets in Tokyo offer non-resident borrowers access to huge long term funds at highly competitive rates. However, samurai, shogun and shibosai bonds are still heavily regulated by comparison with their Eurobond counterparts. Additionally, substantial costs are incurred for small issues, especially by small borrowers unfamiliar to Japanese institutions. Thus the advent of the deregulated Euroyen market has effectively limited the samurai bond market.

The Asian–Pacific offshore bond markets in Hong Kong and Singapore are in essence an extension of the Euromarket into the region. They appeal to lesser known Asian–Pacific companies, or even to well known companies that are borrowing relatively small sums. Japan and Australia and, to a much smaller degree, New Zealand, Hong Kong, China and South Korea are major borrowers in the Asian dollar bond markets. Hong Kong is cost-effective for such borrowings, and Singapore is even more so. Shorter term and floating rate issues, generally between $50 million and $150 million, have proved popular in both centres.

Two further factors that are important to the fortunes of the Asian–Pacific offshore bond market are the concentration of subsidiaries and branches of Japanese financial institutions, and the emergence of Japanese corporate borrowers in these centres. While the presence of Japanese financial institutions in Hong Kong and Singapore has been important, not least in providing the necessary core of demand for longer term bonds, Japanese corporations practising zai-teku have increasingly featured in convertible and warrant bonds issued in these centres. Japanese overseas subsidiaries and Japanese merchant banks in Hong Kong vie to be underwriters of international bonds. Branches of Japanese city banks cannot underwrite these issues. This partly explains why Japanese bond issues offshore in Asia have been more active in Hong Kong than in Singapore. Hong Kong has almost all the international securities houses and fund managers. Many of the two hundred and eighty deposit-taking companies in Hong Kong are Japanese merchant banks and securities trading institutions, which were attracted to Hong Kong because of the original concentration of financial institutions there, and because of its deregulated environment. As the fund management industry grows in Singapore and as new tax incentives take effect, more Japanese securities houses will be attracted to Singapore as well. Hong Kong and Singapore also benefit from their linkages with the Euromarkets. Placement and trading of international bonds can be moved easily between their time zones, given the global distribution of branches and subsidiaries of banks and securities houses. Finally, there has been an increase in the liquidity of international bonds traded in Hong Kong and Singapore because of the massive trading of such bonds in Tokyo.

If securities-related business were permitted in the Tokyo offshore market this would have a significant effect, particularly on Hong Kong. For this to happen, there would have to be a resolution of the remaining differences between Japanese banks and securities houses. Conceivably, both banks and securities houses in the Tokyo offshore market would be permitted to underwrite and trade in offshore bonds in a relatively deregulated setting. Offshore bond issues would continue to be restricted to non-residents and foreign subsidiaries of Japanese corporations. The most vulnerable target of this restriction would be the offshore bond issues of Japanese corporations in the Euromarket and the other Asian offshore markets. This could be accompanied by increased funding of such issues by Japanese financial institutions. However, while some loss would be inevitable, permitting securities business in the Tokyo offshore market would not of itself seriously jeopardise the offshore bond markets of Hong Kong and Singapore in the long term.

In the first place, the smaller regional companies would still find Hong Kong or Singapore much more familiar and closer to them, places where they could get a better hearing. Second, all other things being equal, the international financial institutions find it much more cost-effective to locate in these centres, with their extensive auxiliary and support services, especially for floating rate, shorter term issues, whereas Tokyo will remain a relatively high-cost environment for quite some time. Third, unless it is damaged by the 1997 transition, the strong fund management industry and supporting financial and economic intelligence services in Hong Kong will remain a key advantage in the assessment of particular borrowers from the Asian–Pacific region. Singapore is also beginning to acquire some of these advantages as the strength of fund management is gradually built up by the recent tax concessions and the liberalisation of domestic savings.

Fund management

Singapore's offshore fund management regime is in its infancy. There is a lack of both domestic demand for international fund management and established professional fund managers. The limited range of international and domestic products for investment and trading is also another debilitating factor. However, as Southeast Asian securities find favour with Japanese investors and the size of Singapore's market increases, these issues will become less serious.

Singapore's obvious competitor in this time zone is Hong Kong, with its tax-free, deregulated financial climate, large domestic private savings, and close and traditional ties with city firms in London. It has thus assumed, by default, the role of regional centre for American, British, and now Japanese funds investing in the Asian–Pacific region. As such, it has developed extensive research facilities on equity markets in the region.

Over recent years, rising incomes, increasing public awareness and the global bull run on equities have diverted funds from bank deposits to fund managers in Hong Kong. Increasing political uncertainty has also induced Hong Kong investors to seek safer offshore investments.

Total funds under private discretionary management in Hong Kong are estimated to be about $15 billion. The breadth and sophistication of the unit trust market in Hong Kong are noteworthy. It has attracted large numbers of local and foreign investors. More than three-quarters of Hong Kong's unit trust funds are invested offshore, and opportunities are available for investing in most of the major countries through these funds. Singapore's unit trusts are invested mainly in local and Malaysian stocks. The size of privately managed domestic pension funds in Singapore is less than that in Hong Kong, but the difference can largely be attributed to the fact that nearly all of Singapore's $14.1 billion in pension funds is held under the statutory Central Provident Fund and is thus generally unavailable for private management.

Though Hong Kong is at present better placed than Singapore to compete for the outflow of funds from Japan, this advantage could disappear as 1997 approaches. Singapore's inherent advantages are its proximity to and familiarity with the ASEAN and Australasian equity and bond markets, and its low basic costs. In addition, the recent introduction of concessionary tax treatment for offshore securities trading and the clarification of tax exemption for non-resident capital gains should prove important in attracting fund management units to Singapore. Several Japanese professional and in-house fund management units have recently established themselves in Singapore.

Fund management in Japan has hitherto been relatively underdeveloped and segmented. Trust banks and life insurance companies monopolise the

management of pension funds while the securities houses dominate in investment funds. Trust banks and securities houses, however, compete for the
corporate and household money deposited in trusts and tokkin funds.

Deregulation in Japan has included measures permitting international
professional fund managers to enter Japan. Foreign firms are allowed to
compete for tokkin funds and act as 'subsidiaries' for other financial and
non-financial funds. The likely consequence is that investment practices in
Japan will be upgraded and the domestic fund management industry will
become less of a domain for Japanese institutions only. Increasingly, too, the
stocks of the rapidly growing ASEAN and other Asian–Pacific economies
are becoming more attractive to the flow of Japanese funds abroad. This
channelling of funds is an important source of non-debt financing for the
Asian–Pacific region.

Hong Kong and, more significantly, Singapore are both likely to benefit
from this outflow of investment capital from Japan. Their stock markets
would be greatly strengthened by the increasing presence and participation of
Japanese institutions, whose entry would promote the development of expertise through technology transfer and raise the standards of research, market-
ing and client servicing.

The increased regional investments by Japanese fund managers also
necessitate a constant presence in the region so that ties with individual local
companies can be maintained and strengthened. In addition, political and
business conditions need to be better assessed and understood by Japanese
fund managers. Thus it is likely that more Japanese investment and research
offices will be established in Hong Kong and Singapore. Not only will
employment in fund management and research activities increase, but
entrepreneurs from the region will receive the funds they need to expand
their enterprises.

Futures market

In May 1987, Japan's financial institutions received permission to trade
cash-settled futures and options abroad (including stock index futures) on
their own accounts. This has sparked off very heavy trading in Nikkei stock
index futures on the Singapore International Monetary Exchange (SIMEX).
Transactions in other futures contracts, including Eurodollar, yen and
Deutschmark contracts have increased as well. There will be a further boost
to SIMEX once all Japanese residents are allowed to undertake such trades.

The impact on the Hong Kong futures market, however, would not be as
great. This is largely because futures trading in Hong Kong is limited at present to the Hang Seng index futures contract. Hong Kong's reputation as a
futures centre also suffered severely in the October 1987 stock market crash.

By mid-1988, when stock index trading in Japan is expected to be legalised,
the Osaka exchange plans to switch over from its current futures contract
based on a package of 50 shares (Osaka 50) to trading on the Nikkei 225 share

index. Moreover, the Tokyo stock exchange is likely to develop a futures market on its more broadly based TSE index. Other futures markets will probably be opened in Japan in the next few years, in particular the currency futures contracts and the US treasury bond and Eurodollar futures contracts, which would be natural extensions of existing markets in Tokyo.

Currently, it does not appear that SIMEX's Nikkei 225 is facing much competition from the Osaka 50. The Hong Kong futures market could also be facing competition from Japan. However, the expected trading activities generated by those new contracts in Japan will add much liquidity to SIMEX. Additionally, with the emergence of Japan as a major international financial centre, the general increase in business flowing to Singapore and Hong Kong will be significant, and this is likely to more than offset their loss in market share. Overall, the impact will still be positive.

With financial deregulation in Japan, Tokyo is likely to become the financial centre of the Asian–Pacific region. Once the process of financial liberalisation stabilises, the three leading international financial centres in the Asian–Pacific region will be contending for financial market shares on the basis of their inherent strengths and weaknesses in attracting international financial institutions.

For the Asian–Pacific region as a whole, however, deregulation in Japan is a non-zero-sum game. While it is true that Tokyo's market shares in Asian–Pacific offshore markets will increase, Tokyo's development is also likely to contribute to the growth of other Asian–Pacific centres. The thrust of financial liberalisation in Japan has been to increase not only the efficiency and size of Japan's financial service industry, but those of other Asian–Pacific centres as well. Overall, Singapore and Hong Kong would benefit in their offshore banking, foreign exchange, offshore bond trading and issuance, fund management and futures industries.

Singapore and Hong Kong both have advantages and disadvantages in responding to Tokyo's challenge. Their relative absence of regulation on offshore activities, their proximity to markets in their hinterland, their significant cost advantages and excellent infrastructure make them attractive locations for international financial institutions for both regional and global business. The main disadvantage that Singapore and Hong Kong will face in competing with Tokyo is the sheer size and potential of Japan's financial industry and Japan's dominance in the world economy.

9 The role of the yen in the Pacific region: New Zealand as a case study

Peter Nicholl and Peter Brady

This chapter discusses in turn the roles of the yen in the Pacific as a reserve currency, as a transactions currency, as a financing currency, and as an intervention currency; it then examines the likelihood, and the implications, of a yen currency bloc in the Pacific area. The approach taken is to look at New Zealand as a case study, drawing, in particular, on the experience of the New Zealand Reserve Bank.

Background

It may be helpful to provide some brief background information on the New Zealand economy and the role played by the Reserve Bank. New Zealand has a population of approximately 3 million, compared with Japan's population of about 124 million, and a land area about the same as Japan's. The manufacturing sector accounts for about 20 per cent of GDP, primary industry for around 10 per cent, and various service industries for the rest.

Trade is very important to the New Zealand economy. Most of New Zealand's imports are raw materials, components or capital goods that are essential inputs for New Zealand industry. Its ratio of exports to gross domestic product (around 28 per cent) is relatively high by comparison with those of other Pacific Basin countries.

Historically, exports have concentrated on a fairly narrow range of pastoral products—mainly meat, wool and dairy products. Over the past fifteen years there have been efforts to diversify exports and export markets, but farm-based industry still plays a key role in earning foreign exchange. It also provides inputs to processing industries in the manufacturing sector, and its share of GDP therefore understates its importance to the New Zealand economy.

Other primary industries—for example, forestry and logging, and mining and quarrying—are growing in importance, and within manufacturing there has been a significant trend towards the production of technology-intensive products. The recent discovery and exploitation of natural gas and some crude oil resources has seen a large expansion in petrochemicals and related energy based industries. There has also been a rapid development of the tourist industry. The primary sector is gradually losing its role as the dominant sector in the economy.

On the export side, products have diversified, with pastorally based exports now accounting for around 50 per cent of exports, compared with 90 per cent twenty years ago. Because of this, and because of international market developments, New Zealand's trading patterns have changed. Whereas twenty years ago the bulk of its export and import transactions were with Britain, there has been a significant diversification of its markets into the Pacific region, particularly Japan. In 1964/65, about 25 per cent of New Zealand's exports went to Pacific Basin countries; by 1986/87 this proportion had risen to about 67 per cent.[1]

On the policy front, New Zealand changed markedly in its approach to economic management over the three years to 1987. This was a response to a poor economic performance over the ten years to 1984, which saw real GDP growth averaging around 1 per cent a year, persistent current account deficits, uncomfortably high rates of inflation, and increasing unemployment.

The policies of the past of intervention and regulation of economic processes have been replaced with a set of integrated, market based policies with a medium term focus. The primary aim of policy now is to achieve non-inflationary, sustainable economic growth.

The key features of these broad macroeconomic policies have been a trend downwards in the fiscal deficit, a firmly market based monetary policy, flexible interest rates, and a floating exchange rate. The view adopted has been that, to make the economy more flexible, such key elements as interest rates, the exchange rate, product prices and factor prices should be determined by market forces rather than by the government.

This approach to economic management has brought about the removal of controls on interest rates, the removal of almost all government subsidies and most other forms of assistance to producers, the floating of the exchange rate, the removal of exchange controls, the liberalisation of import licensing, and the removal of a variety of constraints and controls on financial institutions.

In the New Zealand economy the Reserve Bank plays the role of a typical central bank, acting as a banker for the government and the settlement banks. With respect to policy, the Bank's main responsibilities are advising on and implementing monetary and exchange rate policy, and prudential surveillance of the financial system.

While the Bank is the nation's statutory holder of overseas reserves, by tradition the New Zealand Treasury also holds part of New Zealand's foreign currency assets. The Reserve Bank holds the short term, relatively liquid securities, while the Treasury holds some longer term securities. Reserves currently managed by the Bank amount to around $NZ3.6 billion.

The yen as a reserve currency

Important factors that have influenced the Reserve Bank's holdings of yen-denominated assets in New Zealand's reserves portfolio over recent years have been the changed policy environment in New Zealand, and the internationalisation of the yen and the liberalisation of Japan's capital markets. The dominant influence has been the former, but the latter has allowed diversification away from US dollar assets to occur, albeit in a limited manner as yet.

Floating the New Zealand dollar has meant that the Reserve Bank cannot stand ready (as it could under the fixed exchange rate system) to support the level of the New Zealand dollar. This has made the level of reserves more stable and predictable, which has allowed more active management of New Zealand's external reserves. This has led, in turn, to the recognition of the need to manage currency exposure in an international environment of flexible exchange rates. And managing exchange rate risk has seen a diversification away from the almost totally US dollar holdings of ten years preceding the floating of the New Zealand dollar in 1985 towards holdings of other international currencies.

This has seen a building up of yen-denominated assets in New Zealand's foreign currency portfolio. By September 1987 yen assets represented 15 per cent of its portfolio, with the US dollar constituting around 67 per cent. Over the three years preceding the float, yen holdings averaged less than 1 per cent and the US dollar held around 80 per cent (table 9.1).

The currency composition of New Zealand's reserves is influenced not only by the need to minimise currency risk but by the need to maintain an appropriate level of secure, low-risk investments. New Zealand achieves this by holding an exposure of around 50 per cent to a particular reserve currency in sovereign (government paper) risk instruments. It also structures its reserves portfolio to meet a liquidity profile that will ensure that funds will quickly become available should it be necessary. Beyond this, it seeks to maximise yield on its investments.

At present it is still the Reserve Bank's judgment that the US dollar most readily fulfils the investment security and liquidity criteria of this country; and, reflecting this, around 65 per cent of its total portfolio remains in US dollars. All the funds in that portion of its portfolio that must be available within two days are held in US dollars. This reflects the normal settlement period for the sale of short-dated US dollar government securities and US dollar foreign exchange transactions.

Important factors constraining the expansion of yen assets in New Zealand's reserves are the scarcity of suitably developed sovereign-risk yen instruments,[2] and the dominance of the US dollar as the currency most actively traded against the New Zealand dollar. (This factor will be discussed in a later section on the yen as an intervention currency.)

While the commercial bank deposit segment of the Japanese capital markets meets New Zealand's reserve investment needs, the sovereign

Table 9.1 Reserve Bank of New Zealand foreign currency assets (value in $NZ million)

	US dollars				Yen				Other currencies	Total
	Central banks	Commercial banks	Securities	Total	Central banks	Commercial banks	Securities	Total		
1982	62.0 (54.2%)	—	11.1 (9.7%)	73.1 (64.0%)	0.2 (0.2%)	—	—	0.2 (0.2%)	41.0 (35.8%)	114.3
1983	175.5 (26.2%)	442.3 (65.9%)	0.9 (0.1%)	618.7 (92.2%)	—	—	—	—	52.3 (7.8%)	671.0
1984	84.4 (64.6%)	15.2 (11.6%)	8.5 (6.5%)	108.1 (82.8%)	—	—	—	—	22.5 (17.2%)	130.6
1985	408.7 (45.9%)	259.7 (29.2%)	119.0 (13.4%)	787.4 (88.4%)	4.8 (0.5%)	—	—	4.8 (0.5%)	98.2 (11.0%)	890.4
1986	583.5 (38.3%)	468.8 (30.8%)	131.3 (8.6%)	1,183.6 (77.7%)	0.2	62.9 (4.1%)	—	63.1 (4.1%)	275.9 (18.1%)	1,522.6
1987	317.6 (8.7%)	1,342.7 (36.9%)	792.0 (21.8%)	2,452.3 (67.4%)	52.7 (1.4%)	442.6 (12.2%)	52.2 (1.4%)	547.5 (15.1%)	636.5 (17.5%)	3,636.3

Notes: Figures are for year ending in March, except in 1987, when they are for the year ending in September.
Foreign exchange reserves do not include New Zealand Treasury holdings of foreign exchange reserves, which include large holdings of long term yen bonds.

Source: Reserve Bank of New Zealand.

segment at the present time does not. The main reason for this is the virtual absence of a government bond market (particularly in short term instruments) in Japan before 1970. Although the liberalisation of Japan's financial markets has gathered pace since the mid-1970s, government securities markets in Japan are still not sufficiently developed to meet New Zealand's short term sovereign-risk investment needs. Liberalisation has led to rapid development of a medium term domestic government bond market, and there has been a speedy expansion in secondary trading in these bonds; but the same expansion and depth has not occurred at the short end of the government securities market—for example, short term treasury bills. New Zealand's investment in short term sovereign-risk securities at present is restricted to a gensaki transaction (repurchase agreement on a security) on Japanese government bonds. Even with this instrument New Zealand has found it difficult, on occasions, to match its needs in terms of maturity and amount. Specifically, dealers do not always have enough Japanese government bonds to use as security for a gensaki transaction. Also, because of set maturity dates during the month for Japanese government bonds, the required maturity date on a gensaki transaction cannot always be obtained. It is clear, though, that short term government securities are becoming an increasingly important element in the implementation of monetary policy in Japan, and that the market for such securities is becoming deeper.

The continuing liberalisation of Japan's capital markets, the strength of Japan in the world economy, its position as a capital exporter, and favourable time zone considerations, have been supporting factors for the yen to expand its role as a reserve currency in New Zealand and the rest of the Pacific region. However, the scarcity of suitable sovereign-risk yen paper, the highly developed and liquid sovereign-risk sector of the US dollar capital markets, and the dominant role of the US dollar as the intervention currency in New Zealand, mean that the US dollar will probably continue to be the reserve currency in New Zealand's portfolio for at least five years.

Recognising the increasing importance that the yen will play as a reserve currency, New Zealand's Reserve Bank has developed strong financial relationships with Japanese city and trust banks; it has invested in Japanese securities; its staff members regularly visit Japanese capital markets to gain an understanding of the dynamics of those markets, and New Zealand regularly receives visits from members of the Japanese financial community.

The yen as a transaction currency

There has been a marked diversification in trade patterns from Europe to the Pacific region. Whereas twenty years ago 59 per cent of New Zealand's exports went to Europe and 40 per cent of its imports came from Europe, now only 16 per cent of total exports and 18 per cent of total imports relate to that region. The diversification has been in favour of the Pacific region in both cases. Japan has become an increasingly important trade partner, and now ranks as the third most important country (after the United States and Australia) to which New Zealand exports, receiving 15 per cent of its total exports. Japan is New Zealand's most important country for imports, with 21 per cent of total imports sourced in that country.

A similar shift, though not as dramatic, has occurred with private capital flows. New Zealand has been a net importer of capital over the past decade. Whereas these inflows used to come mainly from Europe, today they are increasingly being sourced from the Pacific region, notably from the United States, Australia and Japan.

This trade and capital diversification has seen the US dollar take the dominant role as the most actively used currency in New Zealand's external transactions; it first supplanted sterling around twelve years ago. The US dollar is still the currency in which New Zealand's trade and capital flows are denominated. Detailed information on flows by currency was last collected in June 1986. As table 9.2 illustrates, this showed that the US dollar was the currency of denomination for around 40 per cent of all New Zealand exports, imports and capital account transactions. More recently, informal surveys have suggested that this remains the case today. The share of the yen increased from an average of just 3 per cent of total current transactions (receipts and payments) in 1980 to 9 per cent in 1986, but it gained this increase mainly at the expense of sterling and the Australian dollar.

Information on foreign exchange turnover also points to the fact that transactions in the New Zealand foreign exchange market are dominated by the US dollar against the New Zealand dollar. Of all spot turnover of New Zealand dollars in the foreign exchange market over the twelve months to September 1987, 96 per cent was against the US dollar.

So while New Zealand trade patterns and capital flows have diversified markedly over the years, and significantly in the direction of Japan, the currency in which these flows are denominated is still principally the US dollar, with the yen as yet making few inroads into its dominance.

Under the flexible exchange rate system traders have become more aware of the need to manage exchange rate risk. This has seen the development of the forward foreign exchange market, and the emergence of a range of risk management instruments—currency options, for example. It has also seen traders seeking to diversify the currency of their contracts away from US dollars, though the statistics to date show that this has only happened to a limited extent. Given developments in trade and the capital account and the uncertainties surrounding the outlook for the US dollar in international currency markets, it is logical for New Zealand traders to move towards the yen as a transaction currency in place of the US dollar.

This is occurring in New Zealand, but still only to a limited extent. Evidence that the US dollar is still the dominant transaction currency can be found in the risk management area, where risk management instruments such as forward foreign exchange contracts and currency options are generally only available in US dollars in New Zealand's financial market; it was noted earlier, for example, that of all the forward foreign exchange contracts written

Table 9.2   New Zealand's overseas exchange transactions—analysis by currency

	¥ %	US$ %	NZ$ %	Sterl. %	$A %	Other %	Total %
Exports							
Year ended							
June 1986	7.2	57.1	15.4	6.1	7.6	6.6	100
June 1980	2.5	53.5	17.8	14.9	6.3	5.0	100
Total current receipts (including invisibles)							
Year ended							
June 1986	6.1	49.3	18.3	9.8	9.8	6.7	100
June 1980	2.2	49.4	19.1	16.7	7.5	5.1	100
Imports							
Year ended							
June 1986	15.1	42.6	4.4	10.8	14.5	12.6	100
June 1980	5.8	46.5	3.5	15.5	17.1	11.6	100
Total current payments (including invisibles)							
Year ended							
June 1986	12.2	40.0	4.5	14.5	15.7	13.1	100
June 1980	4.3	40.3	3.8	18.9	18.3	14.4	100
Private capital flows							
In: June 1986	3.5	36.2	39.2	3.4	8.8	8.9	100
June 1980	0.4	30.2	27.4	13.8	12.2	16.0	100
Out: June 1986	4.7	48.5	11.9	6.1	22.1	6.7	100
June 1980	1.7	48.1	3.6	6.6	20.6	19.4	100

Source: Reserve Bank of New Zealand.

over the twelve months to September 1987, 96 per cent were against the US dollar.

The yen as a financing currency

New Zealand has had external current account deficits over the past ten years, and it has had to rely on net borrowing in offshore capital markets to finance these deficits. Before floating the exchange rate in 1985, the public sector (the government and the Reserve Bank) undertook most of the overseas borrowing necessary, but since 1985 the external current account deficit has been financed by a net inflow of capital to the private sector. The only borrowing

Table 9.3   New Zealand's overseas debt, June 1987

	Official debt [a]		Govt corporations		Private		Total	
	$NZm	%	$NZm	%	$NZm	%	$NZm	%
US dollar	7,614	(38.3)	3,482	(49.5)	5,098	(70.7)	16,194	(47.4)
Yen	5,740	(28.8)	—	—	396	(5.5)	6,136	(18.0)
Swiss franc	2,344	(11.8)	—	—	434	(6.0)	2,778	(8.1)
Sterling	1,734	(8.7)	—	—	287	(4.0)	2,021	(5.9)
Deutschmark	1,317	(6.6)	—	—	—	—	1,317	(3.9)
Other	1,156	(5.8)	3,550	(50.5)	995	(13.9)	5,700	(16.7)
Total	19,905	(100.0)	7,032	(100.0)	7,210	(100.0)	34,146	(100.0)

Note: a Government and Reserve Bank debt.
Source: Department of Statistics (New Zealand) 1987.

by the public sector since the floating of the New Zealand dollar has been undertaken to build up reserves and to refinance existing official overseas debt. The latest information on New Zealand's overseas indebtedness (in June 1987) is presented in table 9.3. This table disaggregates debt by categories and currencies and shows that the yen has been an important financing currency of the public sector in New Zealand. The US dollar was the most important, with 38 per cent of total official debt denominated in that currency; the yen was the next most important at 29 per cent; and the Swiss franc followed at 12 per cent. Virtually all private sector overseas debt, though, is denominated in US dollars (71 per cent of the total), with only 6 per cent denominated in yen.

What is interesting about the statistics is that, even in private sector borrowing, the yen has not as yet played a significant financing role. The main reason for this appears to be the preference of the New Zealand corporate sector for borrowing short term (up to three years) rather than longer term. The best vehicles for doing this are the developed US dollar domestic and Euromarkets. As well, from the perspective of managing currency risk, New Zealand corporate institutions want to borrow in the currencies in which their revenues and assets are denominated. With the US dollar still the dominant currency in which assets and export revenues are denominated, the natural currency to borrow in is the US dollar. Another factor is the widespread perception over the past three years that the yen has been undervalued in international currency markets and the US dollar overvalued. Even though interest rate differentials favoured borrowing in yen, private sector borrowers in New Zealand were wary of having their liabilities denominated in a potentially strengthening currency.

The public sector was borrowing in yen well before the 1984–87 period. During the middle to late 1970s and early 1980s it borrowed in yen to support the New Zealand dollar under the fixed exchange rate regime. Official borrowing was long term, and was undertaken with the aim of spreading exposure across a number of currencies. The opportunity to gain access to

Japan's capital markets during the 1970s was taken up by the New Zealand government when it was found that New Zealand could borrow large amounts through yen bond issues at consistently fine rates. This form of borrowing met the needs of the public sector under the fixed exchange rate regime.

New Zealand's experience implies that a currency's role as a financing medium depends in part, and possibly in large part, on how widely it is used as a transactions currency—in other words, the two roles are closely integrated. In future, therefore, the yen should expand as a financing currency as it becomes a more dominant transactions currency. Support will also come from the realignment among the main exchange rates that has taken place in international currency markets, the continuing liberalisation of Japan's capital markets, and the development of a Euroyen market.

The yen as an intervention currency

In March 1985, when New Zealand moved to a floating exchange rate system, the authorities decided to adopt a clean float where there would be no intervention to influence the level of the exchange rate. It did, however, reserve the right to intervene to counter disorderly conditions. To date there has been no intervention by the authorities in the foreign exchange market.

While the policy is non-interventionist, New Zealand retains the capability to intervene should an emergency develop. This has meant that New Zealand has structured its reserves portfolio so as to provide the immediate capability to support the New Zealand dollar if necessary. In the Reserve Bank's judgment at present, the only currency that can give the Reserve Bank the immediate ability to intervene to stabilise market conditions or to support the local currency is the US dollar.

New Zealand's interbank market is dominated by transactions of the New Zealand dollar against the US dollar. To highlight this, over the twelve months to September 1987 spot turnover of the New Zealand dollar against all currencies averaged $NZ105 billion a month. Of this, 96 per cent was transactions against the US dollar.

With this dominance of the US dollar in New Zealand's foreign exchange market, and with market behaviour that focuses primarily on this particular bilateral exchange rate, the best intervention currency for New Zealand is the US dollar, and this will probably remain the case in the foreseeable future.

In order to retain the capability to intervene, the Reserve Bank has supported its holdings of foreign currency assets with standby credit facilities with the Bank for International Settlements and various commercial banks. Japanese banks represent a large proportion of the institutions to whom New Zealand has credit lines. However, most facilities arranged with these Japanese banks are denominated in US dollars. This reinforces the position that New Zealand has adopted; namely, that the US dollar is the best intervention currency for New Zealand's foreign exchange market.

The implications of a yen currency bloc in the Pacific region

This chapter set out to discuss the implications of the development of a yen currency bloc in the Pacific region. Formulating the topic in this way seems to assume that a yen currency bloc will develop, a view that seems to be shared by the Bank of New Zealand, the country's largest trading bank, whose Economic Department said recently:

> In the past 20 years the New Zealand economy has switched from the sterling to the US dollar currency area. The massive loss of price competitiveness that has occurred in the last three years suggests that another change is occurring. The NZ dollar may be joining the yen currency area, as the New Zealand economy becomes more closely associated with that of Japan, and with other countries whose currencies are related to the yen. (Bank of New Zealand 1987)

It is interesting that so prominent a market participant has publicly raised the possibility that New Zealand has started a change in emphasis that will eventually move it from the US dollar currency area to the yen currency area. On the basis of the data set out earlier, however, the Bank of New Zealand's conclusion that the switch is already under way is premature.

Data from other sources suggest that New Zealand's experience is fairly typical of that of other Pacific Basin countries. Table 9.4 implies that the internationalisation of the yen has been more rapid in the area of capital transactions than in that of current transactions. Even for Japan itself, in value terms the yen was used in only 36 per cent of Japan's export transactions in 1986, a lower proportion than in any of the preceding four years, and it was used for only 10 per cent of Japan's imports. In capital transactions the yen has become increasingly important as a financing currency, but it still plays a very limited role as a reserve currency.

It seems clear therefore that the development of a yen currency bloc in the Pacific region is, at best, at a very early stage of evolution, and that the development which has so far occurred has been very uneven in terms of the main functions that an international currency performs.

We agree with the conclusion reached in a recent article published by the Bank of Tokyo:

> Only when the internationalisation of the yen becomes a parallel process affecting capital and current transactions equally will we be able to claim that the yen has emerged as a currency capable of taking over part of the role of the dollar. (Uchida 1987)

The second area of uncertainty in considering this topic was the meaning that should be ascribed to the term 'currency bloc or area'. For example, the quote from the Bank of New Zealand states, correctly, that New Zealand has been part of two currency areas during its history: the sterling area until twenty years ago, and the US dollar area since then. But the characteristics of New Zealand's links with those two areas, and thus the implications for its economy, have been quite different.

Table 9.4 International use of the yen

	1981	1982	1983	1984	1985	1986
Yen-denominated ratio of Japan's trade (%)						
Exports	33.8	38.2	38.9	39.4	41.2	36.0
Imports	2.4[a]	—	—	—	—	10.3
International banking flows denominated in yen (US$b)						
Assets	11.8	5.7	6.4	18.3	43.1	66.2
Liabilities	7.5	3.6	3.8	13.1	37.3	51.8
Yen-denominated ratio of the stock of international banking						
Assets (%)	—	2.4	2.7	1.5	5.0	9.0
Foreign and international bond issues denominated in yen						
Total (US$b)	3.1	3.9	4.1	6.1	12.9	23.4
As % of total issues	6.0	5.2	5.3	5.5	7.8	10.4
Share of yen in total identified holdings of official foreign exchange reserves (%)	4.2	4.7	4.9	5.7	7.5	6.9

Note: a 1980.
Source: Johnston (1987).

For most of New Zealand's period in the sterling bloc it maintained a fixed exchange rate with sterling, and the bulk of its trade and capital transactions were with the United Kingdom. That type of tight integration harks back to the 'optimum currency area' literature of the 1960s and 1970s, when a number of prominent economists like Johnson (1973), Kenen (1969), McKinnon (1963) and Mundell (1961) examined the conditions that need to hold for a country to tie itself to another country's currency.[3]

The benefits attributed to currency unification included wider applicability of the efficiency gains from the classic functions of money (unit of account, medium of exchange, store of value); the elimination of flows of speculative capital that would relieve authorities of this frustration of their monetary control; and savings on exchange reserves. The main cost seemed to be the loss of policy autonomy. Some argued, however, that if the central country had a better policy performance, and hence a lower inflation rate, this supposed cost could have been deemed to be an advantage also.

The literature about the optimal currency area concluded that the greater the degree of economic integration between the central and the satellite countries, the greater would be the potential gains from currency integration.

The indicators of a high degree of integration include a high proportion of trade with the central country; prices of exports to the central country that are set in the central country and not on world commodity markets; exports to and imports from the central country that are a relatively high proportion of GDP, not just of total trade; and factor markets, especially labour markets, with a reasonable degree of integration. For much of New Zealand's history these conditions existed in the economic relationship between New Zealand and the United Kingdom, and it was only when they weakened that New Zealand switched to the US dollar currency area.

However, the degree of economic integration between New Zealand and the United States has never been especially high and, except for a brief period in the early 1970s, New Zealand has never pegged its currency to the US dollar. It has used the dollar to denominate its international transactions, but, while this has at times had real income implications for some of its exporters, New Zealand has never joined the US currency bloc in the sense of linking its exchange rate, and hence its economic policies, to those of the United States.

Which of these two currency bloc models is most likely to characterise any future relationship between New Zealand and Japan? This question should be considered in terms of the four conditions listed above.

High proportion of trade with the centre country. Although Japan is an import-ant and growing trading partner for New Zealand, it still only accounts for about 20 per cent of all New Zealand's merchandise exports and is fairly lightly represented on the non-merchandise side. In the year to June 1986 Japan accounted for only about 7 per cent of invisible receipts (although the number of Japanese tourists is increasing rapidly, and this proportion will probably grow as a consequence) and about 10 per cent of invisible payments.

Price setting of exports.   Much of New Zealand's trade with Japan is in forestry products and wool, the prices of which are set by international auction (or near-auction), so the gains in terms of price stability from monetary union with Japan are likely to be minimal.

Exports to and imports from Japan as a proportion of GDP.   Total receipts from Japan in 1986 were only about 3 per cent of New Zealand's GDP; total payments to Japan were about 4 per cent of total domestic expenditure.

Integration of factor markets.   The New Zealand labour market is almost completely separated from the Japanese market. New Zealand's labour market has been quite closely integrated with the Australian labour market for a long time, and these two countries' goods and financial markets have become more closely integrated in recent years. Despite this, the interrelationships between Australia and New Zealand are still not strong enough for New Zealand to consider joining an 'Australian dollar bloc'.

There are also other reasons why it would be inappropriate for New Zealand to enter a fixed exchange rate relationship with a yen currency bloc. For various structural reasons, there is a strong possibility that the yen may adjust to shocks that are irrelevant to the New Zealand economy, taking our exchange rate with it, or that the New Zealand economy may be subject to shocks that do not affect Japan.

There are two significant structural differences between the two economies that could create these sorts of problems in a pegged exchange rate environment. First, New Zealand is a producer of primary products and Japan is a consumer of primary products, so that, in general, the real exchange rate adjustments needed for terms of trade reasons are likely to be diametrically opposed. Second, New Zealand is at present a net debtor while Japan is a significant net creditor, and Japan may well be subject to upward pressure on the yen as the income flows from its external assets affect its current account balance.

It seems clear therefore that if New Zealand joins a Pacific yen currency bloc, the arrangement will resemble its present participation in a US dollar bloc — that is, the yen will be the denominating currency for New Zealand's international transactions, but New Zealand will retain an independent exchange rate policy. There are probably forces in international financial markets that ultimately push every convertible 'small country' currency into a currency area which is denominated by a key currency. As New Zealand becomes more closely associated with the Japanese economy, and with other economies in the Pacific region whose currencies are related to the yen, the New Zealand dollar will become increasingly linked with the yen currency area.

The pace of this linking up will depend on the future patterns of use of the yen in international transactions in the region and on the course of the real value of the yen. If the yen continues to rise in real terms against the US dollar, for example, New Zealand exporters are likely to become increasingly uncompetitive in the markets of the US dollar currency area. By contrast, no loss of price competitiveness is likely to be experienced against markets in the yen currency area; indeed, price competitiveness could even improve. This could well see a faster integration of the New Zealand tradable sector into the yen currency area.

To summarise: if the yen becomes a more dominant currency in New Zealand's external transactions, and if it becomes more stable against other international currencies than its main 'competitor', the US dollar, a yen currency bloc will become a possibility in the Pacific Basin. From New Zealand's perspective there is a long way to go before that point is reached.

New Zealand, because of its diverse pattern of trade, is unlikely to be one of the early joiners of such a Pacific yen currency bloc; but if and when the bloc develops and expands, it is likely that New Zealand will be progressively drawn into such a bloc.

10 Japanese financial deregulation and international economic policy coordination: some small-country observations

Christopher Higgins

The past twenty years have seen a marked increase in global economic interdependence. The links between markets and national economies have become stronger and stronger through international flows of goods and capital. OECD countries now export about 30 per cent of their gross national product on average, compared with around 20 per cent ten years ago. Financial transactions take place freely across many national boundaries twenty-four hours a day, and the closer integration of financial markets has gone well beyond the accommodation of trade. In 1960, foreign assets of commercial banks in OECD countries amounted to $16.2 billion or 1.5 per cent of area GNP; by 1984 the figure was $1835 billion, or nearly 17 per cent of GNP (Fukao and Hanazaki 1987).

The move to floating exchange rates in 1973, the recycling of the revenues of oil exporting countries after the oil price shocks of 1973 and 1979, and the scope for faster, less costly transactions offered by advances in communications technology, have brought about innovation and rapid growth in financial markets, particularly in the relatively unregulated international ones. The resulting competitive pressures on financiers in sheltered domestic markets have led them to seek opportunities for growth beyond national borders and beyond their traditional, regulated and segmented spheres of operation. The distinctions between classes of financial institutions have been breaking down, as has the distinction between banking and commerce. This greater degree of internationalisation, integration, competition and innovation in financial markets has been a concomitant to their deregulation. Furthermore, the links between capital markets and goods markets have reinforced and spread the process of integration beyond financial markets, transmitting pressures from market to market, from one national economy to another, and from sector to sector within economies.

The greater integration of economies and markets has brought both opportunities and challenges. The opportunities are for greater global growth and welfare through commerce: for exploitation of national comparative advantage in the production of goods and services; and for exchanging goods and services in international markets. The challenges are in accepting the implications that closer integration has for domestic economic structures and policies. Winding down the classic border trade barriers in the forthcoming round of multilateral trade negotiations is critically important. But of equal significance in today's highly integrated world are the intense adjustment pressures that have been brought to bear on domestic sectors not traditionally involved directly in trade. The days when any activity could remain isolated and insulated from the world marketplace are gone, probably for ever.

That is the underlying theme around which this chapter makes some observations about the policy responses of small, open economies to Japanese financial deregulation and to the international coordination of economic policy. Naturally, the perspective is derived largely from Australia's experience.

The recent years of increasing economic interdependence have coincided with the emerging world prominence of the Japanese economy and, more recently, its rising structural savings surplus, current account surplus and capital flows to the rest of the world. Inescapably, a sequence of Japanese responses has followed, including the deregulation of Japan's financial markets and more active participation by Japan in international economic councils. Sometimes those responses have been rapid and welcome. Sometimes they have been less welcome and slower. The sequence has not yet run its course.

The pressures that link Japan and the other major western countries together in global developments are pervasive, and they spill over to small, open economies like Australia. Such economies participate in the same global markets for goods and capital as the large economies; changes in the external conditions they face, including policy changes abroad, fundamentally affect their domestic economies. The agricultural policies of the United States, the European Community and Japan are a topical example for Australia, highlighting the potency of spillover effects from the domestic policies of others in today's highly interdependent world.

While small economies can seek to influence the policy choices of larger economies, they can seldom be certain of success. Their principal response to greater economic interdependence, and to external pressures, must be to develop adaptive economic structures capable of adjusting to external influences, whatever their source. Larger economies, too, cannot formulate policy without regard to the world marketplace, nor can they insulate parts of their economies from it indefinitely.

The next section describes the linkages through which policymaking in Australia is influenced by the deregulation and evolution of Japan's financial markets. This is followed by a discussion of international economic policy coordination, including Japan's role therein, and what this implies for the policymaking environment of small, open economies.

Japan's financial markets: their impact and policy responses to them

Japan's financial deregulation and development have been part of a global process in which Australia has also been involved. In Japan it has been underpinned by that country's rising domestic surplus of investible funds and its growing integration into the world economy. The following paragraphs make some observations on the main impacts of changes in the financial systems of Australia and Japan, first with respect to the links between markets and sectors, and second with respect to some specific issues arising from the increasing flows of Japanese capital, the greater international use of the yen, and differences in national tax regimes.

Linkages between markets

The internationalisation and deregulation of Japanese and Australian financial markets illustrates how liberalisation and expansion in one market can generate pressures for change in others. There are both similarities and differences between Japan and Australia in this respect.

Consider first developments within financial sectors. In Australia, the significant expansion of the less regulated non-bank financial sector at the expense of the bank sector contributed importantly to the pressures for liberalisation; the regulated sector sought opportunities for expansion and the authorities recognised the futility of focusing regulations on a shrinking proportion of the financial sector.[1] Foreign financial enterprises were prominent contributors to the strong growth of the non-bank sector in Australia.

Similarly, the experience of Japanese enterprises in less regulated overseas financial markets contributed to pressures for liberalisation at home. As their familiarity with liberalised markets increased they became more inclined to favour domestic deregulation, and the authorities recognised that excessive domestic regulation would tend to push financing activities offshore.

Experience in the two economies differs somewhat with respect to the linkages between financial markets and other markets (non-financial services, goods and labour), essentially because there is little parallelism between the Japanese and Australian economies in the distribution of regulated and liberalised sectors.[2] In Australia the entry of foreign banks in 1985 contributed to the subsequent wide-ranging liberalisation of controls on direct foreign investment in the non-financial as well as the financial sectors. The internationalisation and liberalisation of financial markets, especially for foreign exchange, has contributed to modified systems of wage determination and to new institutional forms under the Prices and Incomes Accord, and to a major process of change in the patterns of trade and production. There have already been a variety of deregulatory actions in the markets for other services and goods in Australia, and a concerted agenda for structural reform with a strong political mandate is under way.[3]

To an Australian observer the rigid sectors in Japan seem resistant to change. The flexibility of Japanese wage determination processes and manu-facturing enterprise stands in stark contrast to rigidity of the regulated sectors, including agriculture, land use, the distribution system, and even domestic finance. Haruo Maekawa has expressed his disappointment at the slowness of liberalisation and deregulation in the financial field during his period as Governor of the Bank of Japan (*Institutional Investor* June 1987, p.328). Maekawa was subsequently chairman of a celebrated committee which recommended a restructuring of the Japanese economy (Maekawa *et al.* 1986, 1987). Although progress in implementing those recommendations has been slow and remains uncertain, the analysis behind them illustrates how liberalisation in one sector brings pressure to bear on other sheltered sectors.

The consequences of capital flows

Inter-market linkages have carried consequences of macroeconomic signifi-cance from financial markets to other sectors within Australia, as just described. Can it be said that Japanese financial deregulation and evolution have also had effects of macroeconomic magnitude on small, open economies like Australia?

Although no single liberalisation measure introduced in Japan could be identified as having a major discernible impact on Australia, taken together those measures have reshaped the nature of Japan's capital outflow and Australia's tapping of it.

Japanese financial deregulation has permitted foreign borrowers (including Australians), in both the private and the public sectors, greater access to Japan's savings. Growth in investment abroad by Japanese residents has been mainly in the form of portfolio investment. The more significant measures bearing on that have included relaxing foreign exchange controls, increasing the scope of Japanese trust banks and insurance and securities companies to hold foreign currency assets (and, in some cases, relaxation of restrictions on yen-denominated assets issued abroad), and the development of the samurai, shogun and Euroyen markets to allow freer borrowing by non-residents.[4]

The sheer size of Japan's capital flows means that marginal changes in them may still be large enough to have a major influence in the financial markets of small, open economies. Of course, the liberalisation itself has not been the cause of the outflows: they and, in part, liberalisation have stemmed from Japan's structural savings and current account surpluses.

The early 1980s saw dramatic changes in Japanese portfolio investment in Australia; it increased from $A509 million in 1980–81 to $A940 million in 1981–82, and to $A2658 million in 1982–83.[5] Japan's share of total foreign portfolio investment in Australian enterprises increased from approximately 13 per cent in 1980–81 and 1981–82 to almost 30 per cent in 1982–83. This surge was accompanied by an increase in Japanese investment in public sector securities denominated in Australian dollars (Treasury 1985a: 64–65). The increased capital inflow reflected the prevailing exchange rate expectations and interest rate differentials between the United States and Australia.[6] Indebtedness problems in Latin America, a significant destination for Japanese foreign investment, also enhanced the attractiveness of the Australian market. In 1983–84, a decline in the differential between Australian and United States interest rates and uncertainty about the Australian exchange rate caused a sharp drop in Japanese purchases of Australian assets: Japanese portfolio investment in Australian enterprises fell to $A763 million.

Shifts of such magnitude cannot be ignored by small, open economies, nor can policymakers insulate their economies from such changes. In Australia, the float of the dollar in 1983 brought about some reduction in the volatility of short term interest rates and provided greater insulation of domestic liquidity from changes in foreign capital flows (Treasury 1985b). But such insulation is relative, and policymakers remain necessarily much influenced by external conditions. In a fully liberalised financial market environment the setting of policy must pay particular heed to potential impacts on expectations and market reactions. Financial markets are rapid processors of news, from home and abroad, and expectations of the future consequences of present policies can be reflected in present transactions.

Japanese investment in 1985 and 1986 provides an illustration. There were two very sharp declines in Japanese purchases of Australian-dollar-denominated securities—the first when the Australian dollar fell in early 1985, and a second, larger reaction when the yen/$A rate fell below 100 in mid-1986.[7] The latter fall in the exchange rate essentially reflected expectations—in the light of 'bad' news about external accounts—that wage, monetary and fiscal policies would be inadequate to the adjustment task. In the event, policy responded quickly with action on the monetary front (short term interest rates rose by over three percentage points) and some flanking action to liberalise foreign investment guidelines. These short term actions were taken to stabilise financial markets pending the substantial tightening of fiscal policy in the August 1986 budget and changes to wage determination arrangements. These policy actions had their intended effect; by the end of 1986, confidence had returned and, with it, the interest of Japanese (and other) investors in Australian dollar securities.

It is pertinent that, while the flow of Japanese portfolio investment has been volatile, the stock has remained large. The extent of Japan's exposure in the Australian market relative to the size of that market would discourage very large-scale disinvestments—the other side of the coin of small-country dependence.

This illustrates the proposition that the policy responses required of Australia to Japan's financial deregulation stem not so much from the specific measures adopted in Japan as from the greater degree of economic interdependence and integration between the two countries. In the present liberalised and integrated financial environment, actual and expected changes in exchange rates and interest rate differentials seem more potent than they used to be. This environment calls for steadiness in the direction of economic policies and a flexible response to short term disruptions.

Yen-borrowing and internationalisation

The relaxation of controls governing yen-borrowing by non-residents in the samurai, shogun and Euroyen markets has meant greater flexibility in managing liabilities for Australian borrowers. The relaxation of associated guidelines has also allowed greater flexibility with respect to issue amounts, timing and currency diversification. The Federal Government of Australia and some State governments, public authorities and private borrowers have taken advantage of these opportunities. Total yen-denominated borrowings by the Federal Government have amounted to ¥700 billion, comprising nine samurai issues, six syndicated bank loans and three Euroyen issues. At 30 June 1988, ¥367 billion remained outstanding. The proportion of the Commonwealth's overseas debt in yen was 7 per cent at mid-1978 and 28 per cent at mid-1988, peaking at around 33 per cent during 1986.

Euroyen liberalisation, of itself, represented a significant step in the internationalisation of the yen, but the use of the yen in international trade settlements and as a reserve currency is still not commensurate with Japan's economic and trading strength. The absence of an active market for Japanese short term government securities limits the ability of those who might otherwise hold yen contracts to obtain and exchange liquid yen assets and is a substantial barrier to the development of the yen as a reserve currency.

The importance of the yen as an international transaction currency, which will probably increase as Japanese deregulation progresses, should have a positive impact, on balance, on Australia's traded goods sector.[8] This does not require any particular policy response by Australia, or other small, open economies. However, as Japan becomes more important as a trading partner, and as its currency becomes more widely used in trade settlements, the medium to longer term adjustment processes triggered in the small, open economies will probably become more closely related to trends in yen exchange rates.

To the extent that a relatively greater use of the yen would achieve a better balance internationally between the international role of currencies and the economic weight of their issuing countries, greater use of the yen could contribute to stability in the international monetary system.

Taxation issues

Taxation is an arm of economic policy that can be heavily influenced by objectives that run counter to economic efficiency, and by strong sovereignty considerations. It is difficult, therefore, to conceive a set of taxation policy responses to financial market deregulation and integration that would be applicable or acceptable to all countries. Nevertheless, a few observations relating to widely shared principles can be made.

The trends in financial markets described earlier have seen increases in both the international and domestic mobility of capital and in the range of financial returns and products available to investors. Financial market innovation has also extended to the devising of financing arrangements and instruments that help to circumvent tax liabilities.

Investors and borrowers have become highly sensitive to differences in after-tax returns and to the funding costs of alternative financial instruments. The degree of neutrality of tax treatment among financial products, institutions and markets is critical to those differences and, insofar as tax differences influence market choices, to the efficiency of resource allocation. For small, open economies in the Asian region, which are generally net capital importers, this implies a heightened need for tax neutrality, both within the economy and between the domestic economy and others.

The liberalisation of international capital transactions appears to have produced a tendency for real interest rates and real returns on financial assets to converge (Fukao and Hanazaki 1987). In the absence of tax-induced and other distortions in the real cost of capital, that convergence would improve the international allocation of financial resources and raise the level of welfare. Policies to enhance economic growth and welfare therefore call for more harmonisation of national tax systems and international agreement on methods of dealing with tax havens.

While the pursuit of tax neutrality within an economy is not a new objective, the deregulation of domestic financial markets has given impetus to attempts at domestic tax reform. Likewise, the pressure not to get out of step with nominal tax rates abroad imposes an added discipline on the overall management of the nation's tax burden and on its fiscal and macroeconomic policies generally. This also applies to tax expenditures designed to stimulate a particular activity. Such measures tend to distort international capital flows and to reduce welfare in the country in which they are applied.

There have been recent examples of tax changes being made directly from the perspective of international capital movements—for example, the abolition in the United States, West Germany and France of interest-withholding tax on government bonds held by foreigners, and Japan's decision to exempt bond issues in the Euromarket from withholding tax. These were prompted by the need for bond market operations in those countries to be competitive with Euromarket transactions, where the tax does not apply. Australia imposes a 10 per cent withholding tax on interest earned by non-residents subscribing to Australian security issues onshore, but public and other widely spread securities issued offshore have been exempted from interest-withholding tax to allow Australian borrowers to compete more equally in offshore markets.

Australia has taken a number of other tax decisions to promote its greater participation in international financial markets and to facilitate the development of offshore banking units. These decisions include the exemption from withholding tax of interest paid to non-residents by separate offshore banking units, and the unilateral abolition of branch profits tax and dividend-withholding tax (in respect of dividends paid from income that has borne Australian company tax) in association with the introduction of the imputation system of company taxation. The measures have reduced the tax-induced distortions that used to limit the competitiveness of Australian borrowers overseas and the attractiveness of Australia for foreign investors. There are, however, a number of other areas that may require the attention of policymakers. For example, international differences in the taxation of foreign income can distort capital flows and influence the development of capital markets, and may provide scope for tax avoidance.

Another issue is whether economies which are net capital importers should take a discriminatory approach to the taxation of foreign-owned enterprises and of income derived by foreign investors. Allowing for reactions by both capital-exporting and capital-importing countries, economic efficiency is unlikely to be promoted by such differential tax treatment. Any tendency in capital-importing countries to tax non-residents more heavily may relate to non-economic considerations—for instance, the community's wish to obtain additional revenue from the non-resident presence as compensation for per-mitting the associated foreign ownership and control of domestic resources. Likewise, there is unlikely to be a convincing efficiency rationale for offering specific tax incentives to foreign investors. More and more countries are realising that tax incentives, whether they are applied to domestic or foreign investors, are of dubious merit in economic efficiency terms. Long-run needs for capital are likely to be met more sustainably by policies that provide a stable macroeconomic climate offering profitable investment opportunities to all investors.

For individual economies there is no simple solution to differential tax regimes. Greater international tax neutrality, and reduced opportunities for tax avoidance and evasion, will rest on efforts at cooperation between the policymakers of different countries and the negotiation of double tax treaties.

International economic policy coordination

The role of Japan

Over the past twenty years Japan has emerged as a leading world economic power. Japan's increasing economic strength and its myriad links into the world economy have made it a key player in attempts at international coordi-nation of economic policy over recent years. Slow world growth, the incipient crisis of indebtedness in less developed countries, and the emergence of trade imbalances in the first half of the 1980s have provided a new impetus for international coordination.

Most of these efforts have been concentrated in the restricted international groupings: G–5 and the Summit G–7.[9] It is difficult for an outside observer to make a fully informed judgment, but my view is that Japan has not yet played a role in these and other international councils fully commensurate with its economic weight. There is a loose parallel with the internationalisation of Japan's markets; that is, just as Japan still has some way to go in that sphere, its full integration into the array of formal and informal international economic gatherings also has some way to go. The door is open; most of the reluctance appears to be on the part of the new arrival.

After the Plaza Agreement of September 1985 the United States pushed more aggressively for domestic policy action by the countries in balance of payments surplus by calling for faster growth in domestic demand in Germany and Japan, and for accelerated market opening measures in Japan.

Market opening measures and reform of land use, the distribution system and the tax regime could have important consequences for Japan's structural tendency towards excess domestic savings.

Some argue that it is sensible to invest excess Japanese savings abroad against the day that the returns will be required to meet the dissaving which Japan's ageing population will generate a decade or so out. Others, accepting this demographic point, argue that more of the investment could be in suitable domestic infrastructure, including housing, rather than abroad.

Aspects of Japan's land zoning and land taxation regime discriminate in favour of using land near urban areas for agricultural purposes and contribute to high residential land prices. A feature of Japan's latest medium term economic plan is the emphasis given to reforming land and housing policy with a view to reducing the cost of housing and promoting greater private consumption growth and urban amenity. The economic plan also foreshadows reform of regulations governing the operation of large retail stores and aspects of the liquor sales licensing system. These are seen as the touchstones of reform of a distribution system dominated by inefficient, multilayered networks of wholesalers and manufacturers which limit the opportunity for competition and lower prices, and discriminate against imports. Tax reform, too, may have a role to play, it being argued that Japan's tax structure subsidises savings but not investment (whereas the United States subsidises investment but not saving). The arrangement whereby non-taxable interest could be earned from Maruyū savings accounts, which was abolished in April 1988, provides an example.

These developments are consistent with a much bolder Japanese blueprint for domestic reform which, to the outside observer, seems to chart a sensible course: the Maekawa reports. Land use reform and overhaul of the distribution system are two specific policy actions which Japan's foreign friends argue would particularly help both Japan and them. It is therefore encouraging to see elements of these arguments applied in Japan's latest medium term economic plan.

Responses in small, open economies

Small, open economies are in most respects price takers. They have a significant influence over conditions in only a few, if any, of the markets in which they trade, and little influence on major exchange rate and interest rate settings. To the extent that international coordination of economic policy would reduce international imbalances and promote greater economic stability, it would be welcomed by small, open economies. They would welcome too, of course, the stronger growth that a better balanced world economy would bring.

Nevertheless, there is a risk that policy coordination might have a negative effect on small, open economies. Policy coordination discussions involve a small number of nations, sometimes only two. There is a permanent worry that policy agreements will be reached on a bilateral or very limited basis, without consideration of the consequences for excluded countries. There is little evidence that this has occurred, but if it were to do so third countries would be rightly concerned at the adverse consequences for them.[10]

The involvement of the International Monetary Fund in G-5, G-7 and G-10 activities and the scrutiny of world developments by the OECD and the World Bank help to protect the interests of smaller nations.[11] Australia has also benefited from its close links with Japan, and from Japan's willingness to promulgate Australia's views in restricted forums.

But small countries cannot afford to rely solely on good will; they need to supplement it with other collective international economic diplomacy. A recent important example is the establishment of the Cairns Group of Fair Traders, which has been an important influence in setting the agenda for the forthcoming round of multilateral trade negotiations and in advancing the cause of world agricultural reform.[12]

For the most part, however, small, open economies have to accept that they can have little influence on many of the forces that determine their economic fortunes. These forces include the economic policies of other countries. This raises the question of how small, open economies should react to distortionary policies abroad. To the extent that the policies of foreign governments are of a long term nature, they are just as much a part of the environment that determines the local economy's comparative advantage as are resource and factor endowments: for example, agriculture in Australia and New Zealand has adapted to the European Common Agricultural Policy. Attempts to compensate for, as opposed to adapt to, enduring policies abroad will not contribute lastingly to the small, open economy's good economic performance. There may be dislocation and disruption associated with adjusting to overseas policies, but if the foreign distortion persists, the economic welfare of the small, open economy will be greater and the costs lower if adjustment takes place.

Where the distortions emanating from overseas are of a short term or less certain duration there may be policy moves to be made, but care must be exercised in their application lest the responses themselves introduce distortion and lasting subsidisation. The preferred approach is to apply the developed international 'rules of the game', such as countervailing duties and anti-dumping procedures, which have been developed to combat cases of extreme and unfair trade disruption.

The hope of the small countries is that international cooperation, such as the new round of multilateral trade negotiations, can reduce some of the longer-standing domestic interventions which spill over into the international sphere, and that out of these processes will come strengthened and broadened 'rules of the game' that will prevent new domestic distortions from building up in the future.

One of the great challenges for the economic policymaker is that presented by domestic distortions. The removal of domestic distortions would improve national economic welfare even if it had no favourable effects on world trade or on other countries. Moreover, the fewer the domestic distortions, the greater is the economy's ability to adapt to a changing environment. Yet keeping these distortions at bay, and removing them, is very difficult. It is a problem of implementation, not of understanding. It is a problem shared by small and large economies alike.

The liberalisation and internationalisation of financial markets will, sometimes slowly and sometimes more rapidly, weaken or even break down those barriers to implementation. In Australia, integration with international financial markets has contributed to important changes in wage determination systems and industrial relations, despite deeply ingrained traditions. It is only a matter of time before consumers in Japan stop paying eight times the world price for rice, and before other changes occur, broadly along the course charted by the Maekawa reports. The more rapidly they occur the greater will be the wellbeing of the Japanese people, the small economies in the Asian–Pacific region, and the world.

Appendix 1: Major regulatory changes in the Japanese financial system, 1979–89

1979

January
: Partial liberalisation of the prohibition of March 1978 on non-residents purchasing yen bonds (prohibition applicable to bonds whose term is less than one year and one month).
: Reduction in reserve ratios (100 per cent to 50 per cent) applying to additions to non-resident free-yen liabilities.

February
: Lifting of the prohibition on non-residents purchasing yen bonds.
: Abolition of reserve ratios applying to non-resident free-yen liabilities.

April
: Limits on city banks' gensaki sales expanded.
: Abolition of posted rates in call market.

May
: Non-residents granted access to the gensaki market.
: Certificates of deposit with maturities between three and six months introduced and non-residents granted access.
: Prohibition on short term impact loans lifted.
: Bank of Japan engages in active purchasing operations of government bonds.

October
: Abolition of posted rates in the bill market.

1980

January
: Securities companies permitted to market chūki kokusai (medium term government bond) funds.

March
: Liberalisation of interest rates on free-yen deposits held by foreign official institutions.
: CD issue limits enlarged.
: Japanese banks permitted to make medium and long term foreign currency (impact) loans to domestic customers.

April
: Limits on city banks' gensaki sales expanded.

December
: New Foreign Exchange and Foreign Trade Control Law came into operation (passed the Diet in December 1979).

144

Notification requirements lifted for foreign exchange banks issuing and purchasing foreign currency securities.

Liberalisation of resident foreign currency deposits held with Japanese foreign exchange banks; market rates of interest can be paid.

1981

January   Increase in reserve ratios on foreign currency deposits, differential increase on fixed term deposits.

March   Reduction in reserve ratios on foreign currency deposits.

April   Shortening of time before members of underwriting syndicate can sell bonds.

May   Bank of Japan sells short term government bills directly to the market.

June   Trust banks market 'big' trusts.

Banks market fixed-date term deposits.

November   Long term credit banks and other financial institutions market 'wide' accounts.

1982

March   Voluntary restraint on purchase of foreign currency zero-coupon bonds, with a Ministry of Finance announcement of an intention to establish reporting requirements for holders of zero-coupon bonds to limit tax avoidance.

April   New Banking Law came into operation (passed Diet in May 1981).

June   Permission for life insurance companies to purchase foreign CPs and CDs.

July   Permission for general insurance companies to purchase foreign CPs and CDs.

1983

February   Purchase of zero-coupon foreign currency bonds permitted.

Progressive expansion of CD issue limits over the next year.

April   Banks permitted to sell government bonds direct to the public.

May   Postal Life Insurance Fund permitted to purchase foreign government bonds.

June   Abolition of the rule that short term (less than one year) Euroyen lending by Japanese to non-residents be for trade-related purposes.

1984

January   Minimum lot size for CDs reduced from ¥500 million to ¥300 million.

April   Banks and securities companies authorised to buy and sell in the domestic money market CPs and CDs issued abroad.

	Abolition of the real demand rule for making forward contracts. CD issue limits enlarged.

Abolition of the real demand rule for making forward contracts. CD issue limits enlarged.

Elimination of non-prudential limits on overseas lending from Japan by Japanese and foreign banks.

Liberalisation of rules governing resident issues of Euroyen bonds.

Foreign banks join underwriting syndicate.

May   Legislation abolishing the designated company rule passed Diet.

June   Removal of the ban on making short term (less than one year) Euroyen loans to residents.

Yen conversion limits abolished. Elimination of overall limits on the spot foreign exchange positions of foreign exchange banks.

Financial institutions permitted to deal in government bonds (with remaining maturities of less than two years).

October   Foreign banks permitted to deal in government bonds.

December Restrictions on companies allowed to participate in samurai bond issues and total amount of issues that can be issued per quarter by a corporation relaxed. Reduction also in the required credit rating, reduction of waiting time between issues, and permitted size of each issue raised.

Non-resident Japanese corporations allowed to issue Euroyen bonds in Euromarket under the same rules as apply to issues of samurai bonds.

Issues of short term Euroyen CDs permitted (maximum maturity six months).

1985

February Removal of ban on direct dealing in foreign exchange between domestic banks.

March   Money market certificates introduced for Sōgō Shinkin banks (minimum denomination: ¥50 million; maturity range: one to six months; issue limit: 75 per cent of capital; interest rate set at CD rate—0.75 per cent).

Bank issues of CBs abroad approved.

April   Reduction of minimum denomination of CDs to ¥100 million, issue ratios raised to 100 per cent and permitted minimum maturity reduced.

Liberalisation of required credit rating for issuers of Euroyen bonds. No restrictions on size and number of issues.

Money market certificates introduced for other financial institutions.

Interest-withholding tax abolished for non-resident holders of Euroyen bonds issued by residents.

June   Yen-denominated Bankers Acceptance market established.

Securities companies and banks able to lend using government bonds as security.

Brokering of CDs in secondary market by securities companies begins.

Financial institutions permitted to deal in all public debt securities.

Banks' required holding period for newly issued government bonds in their dealing accounts reduced from 100 days to 40 days.

Permission for foreign banks to enter the trust business (participation to begin in October).

July   Collateral requirement in inter-bank call market dropped for unconditional and seven-day contracts.

October   Interest rate controls on large-denomination time deposits lifted (minimum denomination: ¥1 billion, maturity range: three months to two years).

Issue ceiling for CDs raised to 150 per cent.

Bond futures introduced on Tokyo Stock Exchange.

November   Widening of limits of securities companies' intakes of call money.

1986

January   Bank of Japan begins gensaki operations using short term government bills.

Stricter identification requirements introduced for opening tax-exempt savings accounts.

February   Short term (less than six months) government bonds issued by public tender.

Foreign securities companies join Tokyo Stock Exchange.

Investment in foreign securities by trust banks from loan trust accounts permitted up to 1 per cent of total assets.

March   Bank of Japan begins CD operations.

Limit on life insurance companies' investment in foreign securities raised from 10 per cent to 25 per cent of total assets. New limit on investment in foreign currency assets of 25 per cent of total assets imposed. Limit on investment in foreign securities on a flow basis of 20 per cent raised to 40 per cent.

April   Brokering of BAs in the secondary market by securities companies begins.

Maximum maturity of Euroyen CDs extended to 12 months from six months.

Banks' required holding period for newly issued government bonds in their dealing accounts reduced from 40 to 10 days and in their portfolio accounts from 100 to 40 days.

Relaxation of restrictions on issues of Euroyen bonds by non-residents.

Reduction from 180 to 90 days of time before Euroyen bonds can be returned to Japan.

Limit on pension trust banks' investment in foreign securities raised from 10 per cent to 25 per cent.

Minimum denomination for large-denomination time deposits reduced to ¥500 million, maximum maturity for CDs and MMCs increased to 12 months, and issue ceilings for CDs raised to 200 per cent.

June   Removal of the ban on foreign and long term credit banks issuing Euroyen bonds.

July   Limit on investment in foreign securities by trust banks from loan investment accounts raised to 3 per cent of total assets.

August   Limit on life insurance company investment in foreign securities lifted from 25 per cent to 30 per cent. Limit on investment in foreign securities of 40 per cent on a flow basis abolished.

Reduction in the minimum denomination of short term government bills and bonds from ¥100 million to ¥50 million.

Revision of limits on foreign exchange banks' holdings of foreign exchange.

Limit on pension trust banks investment in foreign securities raised from 25 to 30 per cent of total assets.

September   Minimum denomination for large-denomination time deposits and MMCs reduced to ¥300 million and ¥30 million respectively, and issue ceilings for CDs raised to 250 per cent.

October   Revision of restrictions on foreign exchange banks' holdings of foreign exchange.

December   Tokyo offshore market established.

1987

April   Minimum denomination for large-denomination time deposits and MMCs reduced to ¥100 and ¥20 million respectively. Issue ceilings for CDs and MMCs raised to 300 per cent (abolished for foreign banks). Maximum maturity for MMCs increased to 24 months.

Bank issues of domestic convertible bonds permitted.

May   Ban on trading of overseas financial futures by domestic banks and securities companies lifted.

Minimum denomination for Bankers Acceptances reduced to ¥50 million and maximum maturity extended to one year (from six months).

MOF and MITI request financial institutions to voluntarily restrain their speculative foreign exchange transactions.

Relaxation of restrictions on non-residents issuing Euroyen bonds.

June   Share futures market begins on Osaka Stock Exchange.

October   Minimum denomination for MMCs lowered to ¥10 million. Issue ceilings for CDs and MMCs abolished. Minimum maturity for large-denomination time deposits reduced to one month.

November   Domestic CP market begins operation.
               Expansion of foreign dealers' share of bonds sold through the
               underwriting syndicate.
December   Bank of Japan begins operating in gensaki market with respect
               to debentures.

1988
January   Lifting of the prohibition on non-residents issuing domestic
               commercial paper.
April   Minimum denomination for large-denomination time deposits
               and certificates of deposits lowered to ¥50 million. Minimum
               and maximum maturities for certificates of deposit changed to
               two weeks (from one month) and two years (from one year)
               respectively.
September   Bank of Japan allows city banks to participate in the unsecured
               call market.
November   Minimum denomination for large-denomination time deposits
               reduced to ¥30 million.
               Maximum maturity of unsecured call loans increased from one
               to six months.
               Relaxation of controls on interest rates in the inter-bank bill
               discount market and the unsecured call market.
December   Relaxation of issuing standards in commercial paper market.

1989
April   Minimum denomination for large-denomination time deposits
               reduced to ¥20 million.
May   Bank of Japan begins operating in commercial paper market.
June   Small-denomination money market certificates ('super MMCs')
               introduced with minimum denomination of ¥3 million,
               maturities between six months and one year, and interest rates
               tied to the certificate of deposit rate.
October   Minimum denomination for large-denomination time deposits
               reduced to ¥10 million.
               Minimum and maximum maturities for small-denomination
               money market certificates changed to three months and three
               years.

Sources: Frankel (1984); McKenzie (1986); Nihon Ginkō (1986a, 1987);
             Kinoshita (1987, 1988, 1989); *Zaisei Kin'yū Jijō*, 4 January 1988;
             Zaisei Kin'yū Jijō, 10 October 1988; *Japanese Economic Journal*,
             various issues.

Appendix 2:   Japan's offshore market

In view of Japan's rising economic status in the international economy and its geographic location, the Japanese financial market is expected to develop into an international financial centre comparable with London and New York. This will enable Japanese financial institutions to expand their international transactions and give overseas financial institutions greater business opportunities in Japan.

If Japan's financial market is to become such an international financial centre, regulations on the market must be liberalised as much as possible to make them comparable with those applying in the Euromarket. In this context it is very important to implement special financial and tax measures on offshore transactions, and to institute measures to insulate offshore transactions from domestic financial transactions.

Offshore market transactions are mostly limited to so-called 'out–out transactions', where fund raising and portfolio management are undertaken outside Japan by authorised foreign exchange banks. With the approval of the Minister of Finance, authorised foreign exchange banks can establish an offshore account and conduct offshore transactions such as taking deposits from and making loans to non-residents (foreign corporations, foreign governments, international institutions, and overseas branches of Japanese-authorised foreign exchange banks).

On 1 December 1986, when Japan's offshore market opened, 181 foreign exchange banks were approved to open offshore accounts and three more banks subsequently opened offshore accounts. By 31 December 1988, 191 banks had obtained approval to open offshore accounts; these were made up of thirteen city banks, three long term credit banks, eight trust banks, 56 regional banks, 26 Sōgō banks, six Shinkin banks, 77 foreign banks and two other banks.

Table A2.1 details the growth of the assets outstanding in the Japanese offshore market and shows the currency composition of the assets.

Table A 2.1   Assets outstanding in the Japanese offshore market

End of period	1986 December ($b)	Share (%)	1988 December ($b)	Share (%)
Yen-denominated	20.4	21.8	190.5	46.0
Foreign-currency-denominated	73.3	78.2	223.7	54.0
Total	93.7	100.0	414.2	100.0

Source: Ministry of Finance (Japan).

Notes

Chapter 1

The authors wish to thank Heinz Arndt, Peter Drysdale, Robert Feldman, Koichi Hamada, Chris Higgins, Hayden Lesbirel, John Laker, Ben Miller, Paul Sheard and Tom Valentine for their helpful comments on earlier drafts, and participants for their comments at the Seventh Biennial Conference of the Asian Studies Association of Australia, where an earlier draft was presented.

1 In 1990 the Ministry of Finance announced a five-stage, three-year plan for the complete liberalisation of interest rates on all time deposits: from autumn 1990, interest rates on small-lot money market certificates were linked to interest rates on large-denomination time deposits instead of to the interest rates on certificates of deposits; in spring 1991, the minimum denomination for small-lot money market certificates was reduced to ¥0.5 million; in autumn 1991, interest rates on term deposits with denominations of ¥3 million or more will be completely liberalised; in autumn 1992, interest rates on term deposits with denominations of ¥0.5 million or more will be completely liberalised; and in autumn 1993, interest rates on term deposits with denominations of less than ¥0.5 million will be completely liberalised (*Yomiuri Shinbun*, 18 April 1990).
2 Restrictions on securities companies establishing new branches and their exclusion from the network of bank automatic tellers offset the yield advantages of the chūki kokusai fund.
3 At the recent Japan–United States Structural Impediments Initiative talks, Japan's promise to relax restrictions on public takeovers while arguing for the necessity to restrain leveraged buyouts in the United States is suggestive of the authorities' general attitude to takeovers (*Asahi Shinbun*, 24 February 1990).
4 The authors of the comments in this chapter were the discussants of the papers presented at the Canberra sessions of the conference. These papers comprise most of the chapters of this volume. The discussants were: for chapter 2, Dr Masaru Yoshitomi and Dr Hirohiko Okumura; for chapter 3, Professor John Neville and Mr Tasuku Takagaki; for chapter 4, Mr Shuichi Takahashi and Dr Ben Miller; for chapter 5, Dr Warwick McKibbin and Ms Edna Carew; for chapter 6, Professor Muthi Semudram and Mr Peter Brady; for chapter 8, Dr Ralph Bryant and Professor Tom Valentine; for chapter 9, Dr Syahril Sabirin and Professor Heinz Arndt; and for chapter 10, Dr Ralph Bryant, Mr Dai Lun Zhang, Dr Makoto Sakurai and Dr Yoshio Suzuki.

The precis of the discussants' comments used in writing this chapter were prepared by Colin McKenzie and Ian Collins.

5 Other papers presented at the conference argued that different factors, like the levels of non-trade barriers and the levels of spending on public infrastructure, were also important influences on the current account position (Onitsuka 1989; Rapp 1987).

6 For example, in the McKibbin–Sachs global model a Japanese fiscal expansion equivalent to 1 per cent of GNP would reduce Japan's trade surplus by 0.6 per cent of GNP and have a beneficial effect on the United States trade position of about 0.06 per cent of GNP; it would have a beneficial effect on Australia's trade position of about 0.1 per cent of GNP (see McKibbin 1987).

7 For example, the *Asahi Shinbun* of 18 March 1990 reported that at the Palm Springs meeting between President Bush and Prime Minister Kaifu, Kaifu agreed, in response to United States concerns, to persuade Japanese investors to maintain their securities purchases in the United States market. Naturally, as financial deregulation proceeds, the efficacy of administrative guidance will decline, but there are still important regulatory discretions, like permission to expand domestic and overseas branch networks, that may be used as potential enforcement mechanisms.

8 For example, requests to the Reserve Bank of Australia to publish similar Australian information were refused.

Chapter 2

The author would like to thank Peter Drysdale, Robert Feldman, Hirohiko Okumura, Paul Sheard and Masaru Yoshitomi for helpful comments and suggestions.

1 This explanation was suggested by Dr Hirohiko Okumura.

Chapter 3

1 A short term money market where the transactions are loans with maturities of half a day to three weeks and the participants are restricted to financial institutions.

2 The Sims test involves regressing one variable, y, on leads and lags of another variable, x, and testing whether the leads of x are significant explanators of y. If they are significant explanators, then y causes x. If they are not significant, then y does not cause x. To determine whether x causes y, the independent and dependent variables are swapped in the initial regression. For further details, see Sims (1972) and Harvey (1981).

3 This type of fund is exemplified by the chūki kokusai funds issued by securities companies.

4 Takenaka (1983) used observations from the first quarter of 1965 to the second quarter of 1982. To detect changes in the adjustment speed the first observation used in estimation was varied from the first quarter of 1965 to the first quarter of 1979.

5 More details on these changes can be found in Appendix 1.

6 Further details on the different types of short term government securities that can be issued and some of their issuing conditions are contained in Suzuki (1987, 95–96).

7 For example, at the end of fiscal year 1984 the Bank of Japan held 81.3 per cent of the outstanding short term government securities, the government and government-related institutions held 12.8 per cent, and private financial institutions held 0.2 per cent (Bank of Japan 1989: 202). However, the holding by the Bank of Japan had declined to 58.9 per cent by the end of fiscal year 1987.

8 Broadly speaking, M2 + CD refers to cash currency in circulation, deposits with financial institutions and certificates of deposit issued by financial institutions.

9 Recent evidence suggests that the money demand function in Japan has been quite stable, despite all the domestic financial deregulation that has taken place, and that the interest elasticity of money demand is still low (Corker 1989; McKenzie 1989; Yoshida 1990).

Chapter 4

1 On the indirect financing system, see Suzuki (1980) and Royama (1984).

2 In the case of listed firms, the key banks involved are Mitsubishi Bank, Sumitomo Bank, Fuji Bank, Mitsui Bank, Daiichi Kangyo Bank and Sanwa Bank (known as 'city banks'), and the Industrial Bank of Japan (the largest of the three long term credit banks).

3 The most famous case (but by no means the only one) is Sumitomo Bank's role in carrying out the reorganisation of the failed trading company Ataka in the mid-1970s, when Sumitomo bore some 59 per cent of the company's losses despite having a loan share of about 15 per cent (Sheard 1985: 53–62). Indeed, Kawakami (1979: 55) reports that, when the banks had to write off their loans to Ataka, the other principal banks involved argued to the regulatory bodies that, as the main bank, Sumitomo should bear all of the residual losses.

4 This occurred, for instance, in the case of the failure of Sanko Steamship (1985), Eidai Sangyo (1978) and Kojin (1975). For further details and references on these points, see Sheard (1985; 1986c).

5 Nakatani (1984) was the first to model the main bank's role in this way.

6 For evidence that the main bank receives higher nominal interest payments, see Nakatani (1984). See also Osano and Tsutsui (1985) for some empirical evidence on the operation of implicit long term contracts in the Japanese bank loan market. On the latter point, it can be noted that managers of Japanese firms are often reluctant to reduce the level of their bank borrowings, even when their requirements for funds decline temporarily. When firms engage in such 'loan hoarding' they are in effect making 'unnecessary' interest payments to the banks; but in the explanation proposed here, and initially suggested by Nakatani (1984), this behaviour can be interpreted as the payment by firms of insurance premiums to the banks.

7 Schoenholtz and Takeda (1985) also focus on the informational role of the main-bank system. See also Hodder and Tschoegl (1985).

8 For an analysis of information-gathering agencies, see Millon and Thakor (1985).

9 On the concept of voluntary disclosure, see Verrecchia (1983) and Diamond (1985).

10 See, for instance, Higano (1986: esp. ch.3); Johnson (1982: 209–11); and Suzumura and Okuno–Fujiwara (1987). Tresize (1983: 16), on the other hand, challenges this characterisation of industrial policy.

11 The stance of the Ministry of Finance and its administrative guidance over securities companies and the stock exchanges is also an important factor (see Sheard 1986b).

12 See Sheard (1986b) for a fuller exposition and references to the extensive Japanese literature.
13 In aggregate, banks owned 19 per cent of the shares of listed firms in 1985. Sheard (1986a: 256) found that, for borrowing firms listed on the Tokyo Stock Exchange (first section) in 1980, the bank identified as the main bank was the first or second shareholder in 39 per cent of cases and among the top five shareholders in 72 per cent of cases. It is noteworthy also that the level of corporate ownership in the case of banks was 91 per cent (in 1983), much higher than the figure for non-financial firms of 68 per cent; and that non-financial firms had more than twice as much ownership in banks as they had in other non-financials (Sheard 1986b: 16).
14 See, for instance, Iwata's notion of 'implicit taxes and subsidies arising from financial regulations' (1986: 17–23).
15 An interesting recent development is the planned purchase by Dun & Bradstreet of a 49 per cent interest in the Japanese corporate credit inquiry agency, Teikoku Databank (*Japan Economic Journal*, 29 August 1987, p.3).
16 The Minebea case is instructive because Minebea is one of the few firms that engages in 'aggressive' takeovers; indeed, it was engaged in a takeover battle for another machinery maker when Minebea was the subject of a takeover attempt by two United States and United Kingdom investment concerns. Minebea, with the cooperation of securities companies, succeeded in fending off the bid by arranging a merger with an affiliated company.
17 A recent case is Dainippon Ink and Chemical Inc's hostile bid for Reichhold Chemicals in the United States (*Japan Economic Journal*, 5 September 1987, p.16).

Chapter 5

1 Patrick (1987). The quotation is from his original [English] contribution.
2 Bank of Japan (1986) and Nomura Research Institute (1986: 148). Calculation from individual items was done by the author.
3 ibid. The Japanese resident banks held short term international assets of about $539 billion. These figures are not strictly comparable with the IMF survey data referred to above. The latter should include claims by Japanese banks in the Euromarket.
4 Until early 1986 the Ministry of Finance retained ceilings on foreign security holdings by insurance companies and trust banks equal to 10 per cent of total assets. After that time the ceilings were raised to 30 per cent. Otherwise purchases or sales of foreign securities (and Japanese securities by foreign residents) are subject to no regulation.
5 The financial markets of capital-importing countries must not be completely closed. The financial scenes in Asian–Pacific areas are examined by Cheng (1986).
6 Exports of goods and services, or the balance in its current account; see, for example, Niehans (1984: chs 6 and 10). In the case of Asian–Pacific countries, trade balance figures are good approximations of current account balances.
7 Several participants at the conference questioned the appropriateness of treating bilateral trade imbalances as 'capital movements'. Some Japanese colleagues also registered their doubt on this point. I concede that my usage of the term 'capital imports' in bilateral relations is unusual. What I am trying to do is clearly distinguish asset accumulation through trade from asset allocation through portfolio adjustment. When Japan runs a trade surplus with country A, Japan has provided A with goods without being paid for by the same amount of goods.

Instead, Japan has accepted financial claims on A or financial assets held by A in return, and so Japan is accumulating assets through trade. To that extent, A has been able to consume and/or invest more than in the case of balanced trade; in other words, Japan has provided A with that much savings. Japan need not necessarily hold those claims on A until maturity. By selling those claims to others, Japan can reallocate its asset holdings. These portfolio readjustments are likely to be influenced by the expected rates of return and the risk of the various assets.

8 A much publicised government plan to recycle Japan's surpluses stipulates $30 billion over three years. See later in the chapter for details.

9 At the June 1987 economic summit in Venice, Japan promised to stimulate domestic demand and reduce trade surpluses.

10 The theory argues that a country develops in distinct stages, starting with a low level of income and saving when it tends to import capital from abroad. After this young debtor stage comes the young creditor stage, when it has already paid back its debt and has started accumulating net claims on foreign countries through surpluses in its trade balance.

11 Ueda (1985) argues persuasively that it is large budget deficits in the United States that have been responsible for the bilateral capital flows. His analysis implies that Japanese capital was used in the United States unproductively, to finance budget deficits; it would have been better if the imported capital had found productive outlets.

12 It may be argued that US capital imports have been too large and are not sustainable; see note 11 above, and Marris (1985). If so, it is United States policymakers who should move to correct the situation.

13 In addition there are issues of Euroyen bonds by non-residents, amounting to $15 billion in 1986.

14 It should be noted that official international reserves were only $43 billion.

15 I owe this point to a graduate student, M. Francois Kratz.

16 For example, the papers and discussions at the Third International Conference at the Bank of Japan, June 1987. The proceedings have been published as Suzuki and Okabe (1988).

17 See EPA (1986a) for more details on Australia and Korea.

18 For a detailed examination of the differences in predictions produced by various macroeconomic models, see Frankel and Rockett (1986).

19 Japanese banks are sometimes criticised for their slim margins or for their small capital ratios. But they are thus lending at lower interest rates than otherwise, and I see no reason why borrowers should complain. It is, of course, financial institutions in other countries that are complaining.

Chapter 6

1 The primary source for the 1975 export figure is MOF (Japan) *Yushutsu Shinyō Setsujudaka* (Export Letters of Credit Received), and for the 1988 figure it is MITI (Japan) *Yushutsu Kakunin Tōkei* (Export Statistics on a Certified Basis). The primary source for the 1975 import figure is MITI (Japan) *Yunyū Shōnin Todokede Tōkei* (Import Statistics on a Licenced and Declared Basis), and for the 1988 figure it is MITI (Japan) *Yunyū Hōkodu Tōkei* (Import Statistics on a Licenced and Declared Basis). The figures are quotes from Table 32 in MOF (Japan) *Kokusai Kin'yū Kyoku Nenpō* (Annual Report of the International Finance Bureau, 1989).

2 These figures originally came from MITI (Japan) *Yushutsu Kakunin Tōkei* (Export Statistics on a Certified Basis) and are quoted from Table 33 in MOF (Japan)

Kokusai Kin'yū Kyoku Nenpō (Annual Report of the International Finance Bureau, 1989).

3   All the figures in this paragraph originally come from MITI (Japan) *Yushutsu Kakunin Tōkei* (Export Statistics on a Certified Basis) and are quoted from MOF (Japan) *Kokusai Kin'yū Kyoku Nenpō* (Annual Report of the International Finance Bureau, 1987).

4   See MOF (Japan) *Tsūkan Tōkei* (Trade Statistics).

Chapter 7

1   The 'Big Bang' refers to the radical reform of the securities markets in the City of London that occurred in October 1986. The main changes were the breakdown of the single capacity licensing system; the abolition of minimum commissions for securities business; and the relaxation of rules for stock exchange membership.

2   The national treatment principle means equal treatment of domestic and foreign financial institutions, without discrimination.

3   In order to reduce risks associated with the payments system, the Federal Reserve has introduced a cap policy. The amount of a payment order is capped within certain limits: for example, the bilateral credit limit; the sender net debit cap; and the cross net debit cap.

4   The Fed wire is the Federal Reserve's interbank data communication system: it is used mainly for interbank fund transfers; for clearing and setting treasury bonds; and for the transmission of information relating to Federal Reserve policy.

Chapter 8

The author would like to acknowledge valuable comments by Teh Kok Peng and assistance provided by Tan Ee Khoon and Irene Cheung.

1   Direct foreign investments rose only from $4.7 billion to $23.3 billion. Securitisation also made its impact. Loans and trade credit rose rather slowly.

2   With deregulation, a massive shift had already occurred in the composition of personal savings in Japan by 1988. Savings shifted to insurance (18 per cent in 1988 from 13 per cent in 1975) and trust (10 per cent from 6 per cent), and away from cash and demand deposits.

3   About 30 per cent of 1986 savings are estimated to have flowed abroad. This has probably increased as a result of post office savings (20 per cent of all private savings) and other small deposits losing their tax-exempt status in 1988. China, ASEAN, Australia, New Zealand and the Indian subcontinent will be important capital-deficit areas. The Asian newly industrialising countries will join Japan as important sources of capital.

4   In terms of market value at the end of 1986, the top nine financial institutions worldwide are Japanese (eight banks and the Nomura Securities Co). Of the top thirty, only seven are non-Japanese.

5   The deregulation relates to the relaxation and elimination of restrictions on medium and long term yen lending to non-residents overseas.

6   Singapore's cost advantage was confirmed in a survey of treasury activities by the Singapore Foreign Exchange Market Committee in early 1988.

7   Since 1983, between 33 and 35 per cent of Japanese exports has been denominated in yen. The share of Japanese imports which is yen-denominated rose to 10 per cent in 1986 from 3 per cent a few years earlier (partly because of the decline in the

shares of raw materials and fuels), and in 1988 was 13 per cent. Unlike the dollar and the Deutschmark, there is virtually no third-country trade denominated in yen. Restrictions on foreign exchange transactions (including the real demand rule on forward deals and yen swap limits) were removed following the Yen–Dollar Accord.

8   The yen has also gained greater importance in public sector foreign currency reserves. It stands at about 7 per cent, trailing the dollar (at about 63 per cent) and the Deutschmark (16 per cent): see table 7.7. The yen weight in the IMF SDR basket was also raised from 13 per cent to 15 per cent on 1 January 1986.

Chapter 9

1   1964/65 refers to July 1964 to June 1965; similarly for 1986/87.
2   Sovereign-risk instruments are investments in securities issued or guaranteed by national governments.
3   For a survey of the theory of optimum currency areas, see Ishiyama (1975).

Chapter 10

I am indebted to Paul Tighe for research assistance and to a number of colleagues in the Australian Treasury and elsewhere for contributions to this paper.

1   The liberalisation of Australia's financial markets has been rapid and extensive. In 1983 Australia floated its exchange rate and abolished exchange controls on private transactions. There were by then virtually no controls on interest rates on official paper, and bank interest rates have now been deregulated. Sixteen foreign banks have been permitted to establish in Australia, entry to the merchant banking sector has been derestricted, and Australian banks have taken on an increasingly global orientation. Australia's foreign investment policy now places very few impediments on inward investment. Australia's financial system is among the most liberal in the world, and it has deepened rapidly. The Australian foreign exchange market is already among the top six or seven in the world in terms of turnover, and the Australian dollar is probably the sixth or seventh most traded currency; see Reserve Bank of Australia (1987).
2   The more flexible and internationally exposed sectors include agriculture and mining in Australia and manufacturing in Japan. On the other hand, the relatively protected sectors include manufacturing in Australia and agriculture and mining in Japan.
3   See, for example, Speech to the Conference of Economists, Surfers Paradise, 26 August 1987, in which the Australian Prime Minister announced that the third Hawke Government would extend microeconomic reform into a broad range of areas, including transportation, communications, government owned business enterprises, education and industrial relations (Hawke 1987). A number of major reforms, particularly in industry protection and business taxation, were announced in the Government's 1988 May Economic Statement; see Commonwealth of Australia (1988).
4   This section discusses Japanese indirect investment abroad, which dominates Japanese capital outflow. There have also been important changes in Japan's direct investment abroad. For example, while Japanese direct investment in Australia has historically been associated with resource developments, more

recently it has been directed to the services sector, especially real estate and tourism. Some aspects of increased direct investment are discussed in Australia–Japan Business Forum (1987), Department of Trade (1987) and Japan Secretariat (1986).

5   The data are taken from Australian Bureau of Statistics (1985–86). Portfolio investment is all foreign investment in Australia other than direct investment, and covers investments in corporate equities and borrowings by private and public non-monetary enterprises and by the general government sector.

6   Treasury (1985a: 64–5). At that stage the Australian dollar exchange rate was administered as a movable peg.

7   This is based on data from the Securities Dealers Association of Japan relating to bonds issued by the Commonwealth Government, public authorities and, to a lesser extent, fixed interest securities issued by companies.

8   Among the possible advantages are those arising generally from currency diversification and those arising in cases where Australian exporters/importers achieve a natural hedge in matching yen repayments/receipts. For a fuller discussion, see Department of Trade (1987: 33–9).

9   France, Japan, the United States, the United Kingdom and West Germany constitute G–5. These countries together with Canada and Italy make up the Summit G–7 (representatives from the European Community also attend).

10 Some aspects of Japan's Action Program For Improved Market Access and of its May 1987 Emergency Economic Measures appeared to be aimed specifically at increasing imports from the United States.

11 The G–10 includes the countries of the G–7 (see note 9), Sweden, Switzerland, and the Netherlands and Belgium.

12 The Cairns Group of Fair Traders is a coalition of 14 non- or low-subsidising agricultural exporting countries (Argentina, Australia, Brazil, Canada, Chile, Columbia, Fiji, Hungary, Indonesia, Malaysia, New Zealand, the Philippines, Thailand and Uruguay) with a common goal of promoting agricultural trade reform. The Group had its origins in April 1986 when a number of agricultural producers from temperate zones in the southern hemisphere met in Montevideo, Uruguay, to discuss cooperation and common strategies to address the deepening crisis in world agricultural trade. The first full meeting of the Group at Ministerial level was convened by the Australian Government and held at Cairns in August 1986. The Group resolved to ensure that agricultural trade issues be given a high priority in the Uruguay Round of multilateral trade negotiations. Largely through the Group's efforts, the need to address the problems of agricultural trade has subsequently been recognised at the Venice and Toronto summit meetings of the heads of government of the G–7 countries and at ministerial level meetings of the OECD.

Bibliography

Akiyama, A. (1987) 'Deregulation of Financial Instruments Part 1' *FAIR Fact Series Japan's Financial Markets* 10

Aoki, T. and Miyachi, K. (1987) 'Corporate bond market part 1' *FAIR Fact Series Japan's Financial Markets* 4

Arai, A. (1986) 'Bond Rating Organizations: Japan, Foreign Firms Compete for Niche in Developing Field' *Japan Economic Journal* 29 November, pp.28–31

Argy, V. (1987) 'International Financial Liberalisation—The Australian and Japanese Experiences Compared' *Monetary and Economic Studies* 5, 1, pp.105–163

—— (1989) 'International Financial Deregulation—Some Macroeconomic Implications' *Pacific Economic Papers* 168, Australia–Japan Research Centre, Australian National University (February)

Arndt, S.W. and Richardson, J.D. (1987) 'Real–Financial Linkages Among Open Economies' Working Paper No. 2230, National Bureau of Economic Research, Cambridge, Massachusetts (May)

Asako, K. and Uchino, Y. (1987) 'Nihon no Ginkō Kashidashi Shijō' (Japan's Bank Loan Market) *Kin'yū Kenkyū* 6, 1, (May); English translation in *Monetary and Economic Studies* 5, 1 (May 1987)

Australian Bureau of Statistics (1985–86) *Foreign Investment, Australia (Preliminary)* Canberra: Australian Government Publishing Service

Australia–Japan Business Forum (1987) *Report of the AJBF Economic Survey Mission to Japan, June 1987* Canberra: Australia–Japan Business Forum

Bank of Japan (1986a) *Waga Kuni no Kin'yū Seido* (Japan's Financial System) Tokyo: Bank of Japan

—— (1986b) *Chōsa Geppō* (May)

—— (1986c) *Kokusai Hikaku Tōkei* (Statistics on International Comparisons) Tokyo: Bank of Japan (June)

—— (1987a) *Chōsa Geppō* (May)

—— (1987b) 'Showa 61 nen no Shikin Junkan' (Flow of Funds in 1986) *Chōsa Geppō* (June)

—— (1988a) *Chōsa Geppō* (June)

—— (1988b) *Chōsa Geppō* (May)

—— (1989a) *Chōsa Geppō* (May)

—— (1989b) *Economic Statistics Annual 1988* Tokyo: Research and Statistics Department, Bank of Japan

Benston, G. ed. (1986) *Ensuring the Safety and Soundness of the Nation's Banking System* Boston: MIT Press

BIS (1986) (*Recent Innovations in International Banking*) Basel: Bank for International Settlements (BIS)

Business Tokyo (1987) 'M&A Japanese-style' *Business Tokyo*, September, pp.8–15

Cheng, H.S. ed. (1986) *Financial Policy and Reform in Pacific Basin Countries*, Lexington, Mass.: Lexington Books

Chochiku Kōhō Chūō Iinkai (1989) *Chochiku ni Kansuru Seron Chōsa* (Public Opinion Poll Relating to Savings) Tokyo: Bank of Japan

Chōsa (1986) 'Henbō Suru Kigyō Kin'yū: Senshin 4 Kakoku no Genjō ni Tsuite' (Changing Corporate Finance: on the Present Situation in Four Developed Countries) *Nihon Kaihatsu Ginkō* 95, pp.1–107

Commonwealth of Australia (1988) *Economic Statement May 1988* Canberra: Australian Government Publishing Service

Corker, R. (1989) 'Wealth, Financial Liberalisation and the Demand for Money in Japan' IMF Working Paper WP/89/85, Washington DC

Corrigan, G. (1982) 'Are Banks Special?' *Annual Report* Federal Reserve Bank of Minneapolis

—— (1987) 'Financial Market Structure: A Longer View' *Annual Report* Federal Reserve Bank of New York

Danker, D.J. (1983) Foreign Exchange Intervention, Japanese Money Markets and the Value of the Yen: A Portfolio Analysis, doctoral thesis, Yale University

Department of Statistics, New Zealand (1987) *New Zealand's Long Term Overseas Debt Statistics* Wellington (October)

Department of Trade Australia (1987) 'The Liberalisation of Japanese Financial Markets and Internationalisation of the Yen: Progress, Prospects and Some Trade Implications for Australia' Trade and Research Policy Discussion Paper No. 3, Department of Trade, Canberra

Despres, E. et al. (1966) *The Dollar and World Liquidity: A Minority View* Washington DC: Brookings Institution

Diamond, D.W. (1984) 'Financial Intermediation and Delegated Monitoring' *Review of Economic Studies* 51, 3, pp.393–414

—— (1985) 'Optimal Release of Information by Firms' *Journal of Finance* 40, 4, pp.1071–94

Economics Department, Bank of New Zealand (1987) *New Zealand Economic Indicators* Wellington (October)

Eken, S. (1984) 'Integration of Domestic and International Financial Markets: The Japanese Experience' *IMF Staff Papers* 31, 3, pp.399–548

EPA (Economic Planning Agency) (1986a) 'Sekai Keizai Moderu ni Yoru Seisaku Simureishon Kenkyū' (A Study in Policy Simulation Using the World Economic Model) *Keizai Bunseki* 102 (February)

—— (1986b) *Proceedings of the EPA International Symposium on International Policy Coordination of March 1986* Tokyo: Economic Research Institute, Economic Planning Agency, Japan (March)

Euromoney (1986) 'Japan Prepares for a Takeover Splurge' Euromoney (supplement) July, p.32

Fair, R.C. and Jaffee, D.M. (1972) 'Methods of Estimation for Markets in Disequilibrium' *Econometrica* 40 (May)

Feldman, R.A. (1986) *Japanese Financial Markets: Deficits, Dilemmas and Deregulation* Cambridge, Mass.: MIT Press

Fingleton, E. (1986) 'Zaiteku Zooms into the Unknown' *Euromoney*, November, pp.35–52

Frankel, J.A. (1984) 'The Yen/Dollar Agreement: Liberalising Japanese Capital

Markets' *Policy Analyses in International Economics* 9, Institute for International Economics, Washington DC

—— (1987) 'International Capital Flows and Domestic Economic Policies' Working Paper No. 2210, National Bureau of Economic Research, Cambridge, Massachusetts

Frankel, J.A. and Rockett, K.A. (1986) 'International Macroeconomic Policy Coordination when Policy-makers Disagree on the Model' Working Paper No. 2059, National Bureau of Economic Research, Cambridge, Massachusetts

Fujii, M. and Ueda K. (1986) Japanese Capital Outflows: 1971 to 1985, mimeo, Ministry of Finance, Tokyo

Fukao, M. and Hanazaki M. (1987) 'Internationalisation of Financial Markets and the Allocation of Capital' *OECD Economic Studies* 8 (Spring) pp.35–92

Fukao, M. and Okubo, T. (1984), 'International Linkage of Interest Rates: The Case of Japan and the United States' *International Economic Review*, 25, 1, pp.193–207

Fukuzawa, T. (1987) 'Deregulation of Financial Market Segmentation Part 1' *FAIR Fact Series, Japan's Financial Markets* 13

Furukawa, A. (1979) 'Fukinkō Bunseki to Nippon no Kashidashi Shijō (Disequilibrium Analysis and the Japanese Loan Market) *Kikan Riron Keizaigaku* 30, 2 (August)

Goldenberg, S. (1986) *Trading: Inside the World's Leading Stock Exchanges* New York: Harcourt Brace Jovanovich

Gyōten, T. (1987) 'Internationalisation of the Yen: Its Implications for the US–Japan Relationship' in H.T. Patrick and R. Tachi (eds) *Japan and the United States Today: Exchange Rates, Macroeconomic Policies and Financial Market Innovations* New York: Columbia University Press

Harvey, A.C. (1981) *The Econometric Analysis of Time Series* Deddington, Oxford: Philip Allan

Hawke, R.J. (1987) 'Issues of Economic Management' *Economic Papers* 6, 2, pp.100–106

Hicks, J.R. (1974) *The Crisis in Keynesian Economics* Oxford: Basil Blackwell (the Yrjo Jahnssan Lectures)

Higano, M. (1986) *Kin'yū Kikan no Shinsa Nōryoku (The Screening Capacity of Financial Institutions)* Tokyo: Tōkyō Daigaku Shuppankai

Hodder, J.E. and Tschoegl, A.E. (1985) 'Some Aspects of Japanese Corporate Finance' *Journal of Financial and Quantitative Analysis* 20, 2, pp.173–91

Holderness, C.G. and Sheehan, D.P. (1985) 'Raiders or Saviors? The Evidence on Six Controversial Investors' *Journal of Financial Economics* 14, 4, pp.555–79

Horioka, C.Y. (1986) 'Why is Japan's Private Savings Rate so High?' *Finance and Development* 23, 4, pp.22–25

—— (1990) 'Why is Japan's Household Saving Rate so High? A Literature Survey' *Journal of the Japanese and International Economies* 4, 1 (March)

Horiuchi, A. (1987) 'Liberalisation of Financial Markets and the Volatility of Exchange Rates: The Experience of the Japanese Yen since 1980' Discussion Paper No. 87–F–1, Faculty of Economics, University of Tokyo

Horne, J. (1985) *Japan's Financial Markets: Conflict and Consensus in Policymaking* Sydney: Allen & Unwin

Hughes, S. (1987) 'Zaiteku—Beating the Yen' *Australian Financial Review* 10 August, p.10

Ikeo, K. (1985) *Nippon no Kin'yū Shijō to Soshiki—Kin'yū no Mikuro Keizaigaku (The Japanese Financial Market and its Organisation—The Microeconomics of Money and Banking)* Tokyo: Tōyō Keizai Shinpōsha

IMF (International Monetary Fund) (1986) *International Capital Markets* (December)

Ishiyama, Y. (1975) 'The Theory of Optimum Currency Areas: A Survey' *IMF Staff Papers* 22, pp.344–83

Ito, T. (1983) 'Capital Controls and Covered Interest Parity' Working Paper No. 1187, National Bureau of Economic Research, Cambridge, Massachusetts
—— (1985) *Fukinkō no Keizai Bunseki—Riron to Jishō* (Economic Analysis of Disequilibrium—Theory and Empirical Analysis) Tokyo: Tōyō Keizai Shinpōsha
—— (1986) 'Use of (Time Domain) Vector Autoregressions to Test Uncovered Interest Rate Parity' in J.H. Makin and S. Royama (eds) *Nichibei Kin'yū Sōgo Izon Kankei ni Kansuru Kenkyū* (Research on the Mutually Dependent Financial Relationship between Japan and the United States) Tokyo: Sōgō Kenkyū Kaihatsu Kikō
Ito, T. and Ueda, K. (1981) 'Tests of the Equilibrium Hypothesis in Disequilibrium Econometrics: An International Comparison of Credit Rationing' *International Economic Review* 22 (October)
Ito, T. and Ueda, K. (1982) 'Kashidashi Kinri no Kakaku Kinō ni Tsuite—Shikin Kashidashi Shijō ni Okeru Kinkō Kasetsu no Kenshō' (Tests of the Equilibrium Hypothesis in the Japanese Business Loan Market) *Kikan Riron Keizaigaku* 33, 1 (April)
Iwaki, A. (1987a) 'Companies Increasingly Turn to "Zaitech" to Combat Profit Fall' *Japan Economic Journal* 6 June, p.9
—— (1987b) 'Fund management: Corporations Zaiteku their Way around the Rising Yen' *Japan Economic Journal* 5 September, p.28
Iwata, K. (1986) 'Financial Liberalisation and its Impact on the Japanese Economy' *Pacific Economic Papers* 134, Australia–Japan Research Centre, Australian National University (April)
Iwata, K. and Hamada, K. (1980) *Kin'yū Seisaku to Ginkō Kōdō* (Monetary Policy and Bank Behaviour) Tokyo: Tōyō Keizai Shinpōsha
Jaffee, D.M. and Modigliani, F. (1969) 'A Theory and Test of Credit Rationing' *American Economic Review* 59 (December)
Japan Secretariat (1986) Japan as a Capital Exporter, Japan Secretariat Research Paper, Department of Foreign Affairs, Canberra
Jensen, M.C. and Ruback, R.S. (1983) 'The Market for Corporate Control: the Scientific Evidence' *Journal of Financial Economics* 11, pp.5–50
Johnson, C. (1982) *MITI and the Japanese Miracle* Stanford: Stanford University Press
Johnson, H.G. (1973) 'The Exchange Rate Question for a United Europe: Internal Flexibility and External Rigidity versus External Flexibility and Internal Rigidity' in A.K. Swoboda (ed.) *Europe and the Evolution of the International Monetary System* Leiden: International Center for Monetary and Banking Studies, International Economic Series vol. 1, pp.81–92
Johnston, B. (1987) 'Liberalisation of Japan's Financial Markets Has Important Impact on International Transactions' *IMF Survey* 28 September, pp.277–81
Kaizuka, K. and Onodera, H. (1974) 'Shin'yō Wariate ni Tsuite' (On Credit Rationing) *Keizai Kenkyū* 25, 1 (January)
Kaufman, G. (1986) *The US Financial System* New York: Prentice–Hall
Kawakami T. (1979) *Henbō Suru Sumitomo Ginkō no Sugao* (The Real Face of the Changing Sumitomo Bank), Tokyo, Nihon Jitsugyō
Kenen, P.B. (1969) 'The Theory of Optimum Currency Areas: An Eclectic View' in R.A. Mundell and A.K. Swoboda (eds) *Monetary Problems of the International Economy* Chicago: University of Chicago Press, pp.41–60
Kinoshita, K. (1987) 'Ōguchi Teiki Yokin Nado no Toriatsukai o Isso Danryokuka' (Increased Flexibility of Large-denomination Deposits)' *Kin'yū Zaisei Jijō* 29 June
Komiya, R. and Suda, M. (1983) *Gendai Kokusai Kin'yūron-Rekishi Seisakuhen* (Contemporary International Finance—Volume on History and Policy) Tokyo: Nihon Keizai Shimbunsha
Kuroda A. (1987) 'Kaigai Shihon Chōtatsu no Zōka to Kokunai Shasai Shijō Kaikaku

no Hitsuyōsei' (Increase in Overseas Capital Raisings and the Necessity for Reform of the Domestic Bond Market) *Gekkan NIRA* August, pp.12–15

Kuroda, I. (1979) 'Waga Kuni ni Okeru Kashidashi Kinri no Kettei ni Tsuite' (The Mechanism of Bank-loan Rates Determination in Japan) *Kin'yū Kenkyū Shiryō* 2 (April)

Kurosawa, Y. (1986) 'Corporate Credit Rating in Japan' *Journal of Japanese Trade and Industry* May–June, pp.17–19

Maekawa, H. et al. (1986) *Report of the Advisory Group on Economic Structural Adjustment for International Harmony* Tokyo: Naikaku Kanbō Naikaku Naisei Shingishitsu (April)

—— (1987) *Report of the Economic Council's Special Committee on Restructuring* Tokyo: Naikaku Kanbō Naikaku Naisei Shingishitsu (April)

Magee, S.P. and Rao, R.K.S. (1980) 'Vehicle and Nonvehicle Currencies in International Trade' *American Economic Review* 70 (May), pp.368–73

Manne, H. (1965) 'Mergers and the Market for Corporate Control' *Journal of Political Economy* 73, pp.110–20

Marris, S. (1985) *Deficits and the Dollar: The World Economy at Risk* Washington DC: Institute for International Economics

McKenzie, C.R. (1986a) The Impact of Financial Deregulation in Australia and Japan on Australia–Japan Financial Flows, mimeo, Department of Economics, Australian National University

—— (1986b) Issues in Foreign Exchange Policy in Japan: Sterilized Intervention, Currency Substitution and Financial Liberalisation, doctoral thesis, Australian National University

—— (1988) Stable Shareholdings, Customer Relations and Japanese Life Insurance Companies, mimeo, Department of Economics, Australian National University

—— (1989) Currency Substitution in Japan, mimeo, Department of Economics, Osaka University

McKibbin, W.J. (1987) 'Policy Analysis with the MSG2 Model', Research Discussion Paper No. 8712, Reserve Bank of Australia, Sydney

McKinnon, R.I. (1963) 'Optimum Currency Areas' *American Economic Review* 53 (September), pp.717–25

—— (1979) *Money in International Exchange* New York: Oxford University Press

—— (1982) 'Currency Substitution and Instability in the World Dollar Standard' *American Economic Review* 72, 3, pp.320–33

Millon, M.H. and Thakor, A.V. (1985) 'Moral Hazard and Information Sharing: a Model of Financial Information Gathering Agencies' *Journal of Finance* 40, 5, pp.1403–22

Ministry of Finance (1987) *Kokusai Kin'yū Kyoku Nenpō* (Annual Report by the International Finance Bureau) Tokyo

Mirus, R. and Yeung, B. (1987) 'The Relevance of the Invoicing Currency in Intra-Firm Trade Transactions' *Journal of International Money and Finance* 6, pp.449–64

Mundell, R.A. (1961) 'A Theory of Optimum Currency Areas' *American Economic Review* 51 (September), pp.657–65

Mutoh, T. and Hamada K. (1984) 'International Short-term Capital Flows and the Foreign Exchange Rate: Japan 1973–80' *Economic Studies Quarterly* 35, 2, pp.95–115

Nakatani, I. (1984) 'The Economic Role of Financial Corporate Grouping' in M. Aoki (ed.) *The Economic Analysis of the Japanese Firm* Amsterdam: Elsevier Science Publishers, pp.227–58

Nasu, M. (1987) *Gendai Nippon no Kin'yū Kōzō* (Financial Structure of Present-day Japan) Tokyo: Tōyō Keizai Shinpōsha

Niehans, J. (1984) *International Monetary Economics* Baltimore: Johns Hopkins University Press

Nomura Research Institute (1986) *10 Nengo no Sekai Keizai to Kin'yū Shihon Shijo* (The World Economy and Financial–Capital Markets Ten Years Hence) Tokyo

OECD (Organisation for Economic Corporation and Development) (1988) *Economic Outlook* No.43, Paris: OECD

Ōkurashō Zaisei Kin'yū Kenkyūsho Kenkyūbu (1987) *Kōzō Henka no Kigyō Kin'yū ni Ataeru Eikyō* (The Impact of Structural Change on Corporate Finance) Tokyo: Ōkurashō Insatsukyoku

Onitsuka, Y. (1989) 'The Investment–Savings Imbalance in Japan and Global Financial Integration: Causes and Policy Issues' *Pacific Economic Papers* 169, Australia–Japan Research Centre, Australian National University (March)

Onitsuka, Y. ed. (1985) *Shihon Yushutsu no Keizaigaku* (Economics of Capital Exports) Tokyo: Tsūshō Sangyō Chōsakaī

Osano, H. and Tsutsui, Y. (1985) 'Implicit Contracts in the Japanese Bank Loan Market' *Journal of Financial and Quantitative Analysis* 20, 2, pp.211–29

Osano, H. and Tsutsui, Y. (1985) 'Implicit Contracts in the Japanese Bank Loan Market' *Journal of Financial and Quantitative Analysis* 20, 2, pp.211–29

Otani, I. and Tiwari, S. (1981) 'Capital Controls and Interest Rate Parity: the Japanese Experience, 1978–81' *IMF Staff Papers* 28, 4, pp.793–815

Pascale, R. and Rohlen, T.P. (1983) 'The Mazda Turnaround' *Journal of Japanese Studies* 9, 2, pp.219–63

Patrick, H. (1987) 'Kin'yū Chōtaikoku Nippon' (Japan as an International Financial Superpower) *Nippon Keizai Kenkyū Sentah Kaihō* No. 540, 15 July

Pettway, R.H. (1982) 'Interest Rates of Japanese Long-term National Bonds: Have Interest Rates Been Liberalised?' *Keio Economic Studies* 19, 1, pp.91–100

Pettway, R.H. and Tapley, T.C. (1985) 'Segmented versus Integrated Capital Markets: The Case of Dually Listed Stocks on the Tokyo and New York Stock Exchanges' *Keio Economic Studies* 22, 2, pp.17–34

Poole, R. (1970) 'Optimal Choice of Monetary Policy Instruments in a Simple Stochastic Macro Model' *Quarterly Journal of Economics* May

Rapp, W.V. (1987) Japanese Overseas Investment and Internal Economic Stress, paper presented at the AJRC–FAIR Conference on 'The Impact of Developments in Japan's Financial Markets in Asia and the Pacific' Canberra (November) Bank of America

Reagan, P.B. and Stulz, R.M. (1989) 'Contracts, Delivery Lags and Currency Risks' *Journal of International Money and Finance* 8, pp.89–103

Reserve Bank of Australia (1987) 'The Australian Foreign Exchange Market' *Bulletin*, 14–18 August

Royama, S. (1984) 'The Japanese Financial System: Past, Present, and Future' *Japanese Economic Studies* 12, 2, pp.3–32

Sachs, J. and Roubini, N. (1988) 'Sources of Macroeconomic Imbalances in the World Economy: A Simulation Approach' in Suzuki and Okabe (eds) *Toward a World of Economic Stability*

Schoenholtz, K. and Takeda M. (1985) 'Jōhō Katsudō to Mein Banku Sei' (Informational Activities and the Main Bank System) *Kin'yu Kenkyu* (Bank of Japan) 4, pp.1–24

Sheard, P. (1985) 'Main Banks and Structural Adjustment in Japan', *Pacific Economic Papers* 129, Australia–Japan Research Centre, Australian National University (December)

—— (1986a) 'Main Banks and Internal Capital Markets in Japan' *Shōken Keizai* 157, pp.255–85

—— (1986b) 'Intercorporate Shareholdings and Structural Adjustment in Japan' *Pacific Economic Papers* 140, Australia–Japan Research Centre, Australian National University (October)

—— (1986c) The Main Bank System and Corporate Monitoring and Control in Japan, unpublished ms, Australian National University

Shinkai, Y. (1988) 'Internationalisation of Finance in Japan' in T. Inoguchi and D.I. Okimoto (eds) *The Changing International Context* Stanford University Press

Shleifer, A. and Vishny, R.W. (1986) 'Large Shareholders and Corporate Control' *Journal of Political Economy* 94, 3, pp.461–88

Shōken Torihiki Shingikai (1986) 'Shasai Hakkō Shijō no Arikata ni Tsuite' (On the Nature of the Bond Issuance Market) *Zaisei Kin'yū Jijō*, 8 December, pp.44–9; 15 December, pp.40–8

Shūkan Tōyō Keizai (1985) *Kigyō Keiretsu Sōran 1986 Nenban* (Directory of Corporate Affiliations, 1986 Edition) Tokyo: Tōyō Keizai Shinpōsha

Sims, C.A. (1972) 'Money, Income and Causality' *American Economic Review* 62, 4

Stevens, E.J. (1984) 'Risk in Large-Dollar Transfer Systems' *Federal Reserve Bank of Cleveland Economic Review* Fall, pp.2–16

Stiglitz, J.E. (1985) 'Credit Markets and the Control of Capital' *Journal of Money, Credit and Banking* 17, pp.133–52

—— (1987) 'The Causes and Consequences of the Dependence of Quality on Price' *Journal of Economic Literature* 25, 1 (March)

Sumitomo Bank (1983) *Sumitomo Ginkō '83* (Sumitomo Bank '83) Osaka Sumitomo Shintaku Ginkō Chōsabu (1985) 'Kashidashi Kinri no kōchokusei ni tsuite' (On the Rigidity of Loan Rates) *Chōsa Jōhō* 1155 (May)

Suzuki, Y. (1980) *Money and Banking in Contemporary Japan* (tr. J. Greenwood) New Haven: Yale University Press

—— (1986a) *Money Finance, and Macroeconomic Performance in Japan* New Haven: Yale University Press

—— (1986b) 'Comparative Studies of Financial Innovation, Deregulation, and Reform in Japan and the United States' *Japan and the United States Today* Columbia University, Center on Japanese Economy and Business

—— (1987), *The Japanese Financial System* Oxford: Clarendon Press

Suzuki, Y. and Okabe, M. eds (1988) *Toward a World of Economic Stability: Optimal Monetary Framework and Policy* Tokyo: University of Tokyo Press

Suzuki, Y. and Yomo, H. eds (1986) *Financial Innovations and Monetary Policy: Asia and the West* Tokyo: University of Tokyo Press

Suzumura, K. and Okuno–Fujiwara, M. (1987) 'Industrial Policy in Japan: Overview and Evaluation' *Pacific Economic Papers* 146, Australia–Japan Research Centre, Australian National University (April)

Takagaki, T. (1987) Japan as a Capital Exporter, With Emphasis on the Role of the Private Sector, paper presented at the AJRC–FAIR Conference on 'The Impact of Developments in Japan's Financial Markets in Asia and the Pacific' Canberra (November) Bank of Tokyo

Takenaka, H. (1983) 'Shikin Furo no Henka to Kinri Kinō' (Changes in Money Flows and the Functions of Interest Rates) *Keizai Semina* 338 (March)

Takenaka, H. et al. (1987) 'Saiteki Seisaku Kyōchō no Keiryō Bunseki' (An Econometric Analysis of the Optimal Policy Coordination) *Fainansu Rebyu* 5 (June)

Takeuchi, Y. and Yamamoto, T. (1987) 'Gaikoku Kawase Shijō ni Okeru Yūkōsei ni Tsuite' (Concerning the Efficiency of Foreign Exchange Markets) *Keizai Kenkyū* 38, 2, pp.97–109

Tamura, T. (1987) 'Changes in Corporate Fund Raising and Management: Part 2' *FAIR Fact Series, Japan's Financial Markets* 29

Terrell, H.S. et al. (1989) 'The US and UK Activities of Japanese Banks: 1980–1988' International Finance Discussion Paper No.361, Board of Governors of the Federal Reserve System, Washington DC

Tōkyō Shōken Torihikisho Chōsabu (various editions) *Tōshō Tōkei Nenpō* (Annual Statistics Report of Tokyo Stock Exchange) Tokyo: Tōkyō Shōken Torihikisho Chōsabu

Treasury (Australia) (1985a) 'Japan and Australia—Financial Flows' *The Round-up* July, pp.55–69

—— (1985b) 'Some Observations on the Floating of the Australian Dollar' *The Round-up* July, pp.71–8

Tresize, P.H. (1983) 'Industrial Policy is not the Major Reason for Japan's Success' *Brookings Review* 1, 3, pp.13–18

Uchida, M. (1987) 'The Internationalisation of the Yen' *Tokyo Financial Review* 12, 10 (October)

Ueda, K. (1982) 'Kashidashi Shijō to Kin'yū Seisaku, (The Loan Market and Monetary Policy in Japan) discussion paper, Bank of Japan

—— (1985) 'The Japanese Current Account Surplus and Fiscal Policy in Japan and US' Discussion Paper No. 2, Institute for Financial Research, Ministry of Finance (October)

Ueno, H. ed. (1987) *2005 Nen no Kin'yū* (The Financial System in the 21st Century) Tokyo: Nippon Keizai Shinposha

US Department of Treasury (1986) *National Treatment Study: Report to Congress on Foreign Government Treatment of US Commercial Banking and Securities Organisations* Washington DC: US Treasury

Vergari, J. and Shue, V. (1986) *Checks, Payments, and Electronic Banking* New York: Practising Law Institute

Verrecchia, R.E. (1983) 'Discretionary Disclosure' *Journal of Accounting and Economics* 5, pp.179–94

Watanabe, K. (1987) 'Corporate Bond Market: Part 2' *FAIR Fact Series Japan's Financial Markets* 5

Yoshida, T. (1990) 'On the Stability of the Japanese Money Demand Function: Estimation Results Using the Error Correction Model' *Monetary and Economic Studies* 8, 1, pp.1–48

Yoshitomi, M. (1987) The Internationalisation of the Yen and the Role of Japan in the World Economy, paper presented at the AJRC–FAIR Conference on 'The Impact of Developments in Japan's Financial Markets in Asia and the Pacific' Canberra (November) Economic Planning Agency, Japan

Zaisei Kin'yū Jijō (1987) 'Shōken Anarisuto no Jūjitsu ga Kyūmu to Natte Iru' (Upgrading of Securities Analysts is a Pressing Task) *Zaisei Kin'yū Jijō* 6 July, pp.62–3

Index

agricultural cooperatives, 40
agricultural policies, 134, 136, 141, 142
agricultural trade, 120, 131; *see also*
  primary products
American dollars, 22, 89, 90, 91, 94, 101;
  in New Zealand, 121, 124, 126, 127
anti-dumping measures, 142
ASEAN, *see* Association of South-East
  Asian Nations
Asian countries, 78, 80; Japanese
  investment in, 81, 82, 84, 108, 117;
  trade with, 90–1, 120, 129, 134; *see also*
  Indonesia; Malaysia etc.; Southeast
  Asia; Western Asia
Asian dollar markets, 107, 109
Asian Currency Unit, 110
assets: held in yen, 29, 42, 89, 100–1, 107;
  New Zealand, 121–3; Japan, 28, 76;
    accumulation, 18, 48;
    foreign, 79, 100, 137;
    personal sector, 23;
  substitutability, 40–1; US, 76
Association of South-East Asian Nations
  (ASEAN), 107; borrowing, 109;
  interbank transactions with, 111
Australia: and Japan, 78, 135, 136, 142;
  Australian dollar, 124, 131, 137, 158;
    depreciation, 23;
    floating of, 23, 137
  capital inflow, 18, 107, 136; fiscal
  policy, 137; industrial relations, 143;
  interest rates, 41; Prices and Incomes
  Accord, 135; private sector borrowing,
  22, 109; takeover market, 63; trade
  balance, 17, 84;
    surplus, 78;
  wage fixing, 23

Bank for International Settlements, 76,
  127
Bank of Japan, 15, 19, 29, 44, 46, 47, 99,
  136, 144, 145; influence of, 50, 53;
  Sinking Fund, 53
Bank of New Zealand, 22, 128
Bank of Tokyo, 128
bankers' acceptance, 9, 28
bankruptcy, 61, 72
banks and banking: and postal savings
  system, 31; Australia, 135; bank
  debentures, 33, 46, 50; bank notes, 99;
  central, 16, 18, 22, 89, 100;
    see also Exchange rates—central bank
    intervention;
    foreign exchange reserves, 18, 19, 22,
      40, 45;
    Indonesia, 19;
    New Zealand, 21–2;
    Thailand, 19;
  commercial *see* banks and banking—
  trading; conflict of interest, 38; credit
  control, 15; deposits, 19;
    deposit insurance, 20;
  deregulation, 39, 135; foreign exchange
  transactions, 21, 90; Hong Kong,
  110–13; international factors, 21, 91–2,
  102, 109, 112, 146; investment
  management, 110; Japan, 32, 36, 44,
  46, 60, 66–7, 70–1, 76, 92, 98, 107,
  110;
    abroad, 109;
    as shareholders, 37, 60, 155;
    city banks, 36, 115, 145, 149, 154;
    foreign banks, 37, 146, 147;
    long term credit banks, 36, 46, 86;
    trust banks, 46;

lending behaviour, 15, 20, 46, 47, 50, 56, 85, 92; main-bank system, 16–17, 56, 60–1, 64–6;
monitoring role, 62–3, 71
non-intervention policies, 22;
permitted activities, 15; Singapore, 110–13; technological changes, 27; trading, 36, 37, 107;
see also Bank of New Zealand;
trust, 36–7, 145;
foreign investments, 39, 136;
US, 99
Basel Committee on Banking:
Regulations and Supervisory Practices, 98
bond markets, 21, 23, 42, 58–9, 94, 114–16; Eurodollar, 57, 58, 114; Swiss, 57, 58; Japanese, 114, 144; yen denominated, 42, 92, 93, 94, 144; see also samurai bonds
bonds: convertible, 57, 59; corporate see corporate bonds; government see government bonds; rating agencies, 55, 62, 67, 70; warrant, 57, 59, 60
borrowing, 67, 138, 139; corporate, 56, 62, 63; long term, 56–7; public sector, 40, 138
Brady, Peter, 10, 14, 19, 21, 105, 119
budgets, deficit; Japan, 27, 48; US, 28

Cairns Group of Fair Traders, 142, 159
call market, 9
Canadian interest rates, 41
capital: deregulation, 38; exports, 85, 86; foreign reserves of, 19, 45; measurement, 98; mobility of, 40; regulation of, 14, 19, 38, 45, 98;
capital gains, 43, 116
capital inflow: Asian–Pacific countries, 77; deregulation, 15, 18, 136; Japan, 16, 27, 43, 83, 136; New Zealand, 124, 125; US, 13, 83
capital markets, 15, 38, 55, 60, 113, 133; controls, 17, 18, 40, 42, 63; diversification, 18, 95; maturity transformation, 17, 82; micro-level organisation, 55
capital outflow, 75–83, 158; deregulation, 15, 133; excess, 48, 78, 107; from Japan, 13, 17–18, 27–8, 43, 78, 79, 107, 117, 136
Caribbean, 111
certificates of deposit, 19, 28, 29, 50, 103; owned by foreigners, 42, 144

China: and Hong Kong, 111; and Japan, 78; borrowing, 109; capital deficit, 107
chūki kokusai fund, 9, 15, 31, 34, 37
collateralisation, 20
commercial papers, 9, 103
companies, 48; capital raising, 15, 45, 55; finance, 55–72, 107; intercorporate shareholdings, 63; main-bank intervention, 66; managers, 55, 63, 67, 70; shareholders, 55, 64–5; taxation see taxation—companies
corporate bonds, 52, 57, 66
corporate raiders, 63
corporations see companies
credit: deregulated, 111; rationing, 15, 46, 47, 48, 49, 50; ratings, 46, 67
currency, 73; convertible, 19; for financing, 19, 100–1; for intervention, 127; internationalisation, 18, 41, 93, 95; reserves, 21, 22, 88, 145; substitution, 41, 89, 124; see also American dollars; Deutschmark; sterling; yen;

debenture markets, 23; see also banks and banking—bank debentures
deregulation see financial deregulation
Deutschmark, 90, 94, 113
developing countries, 102; see also Pacific countries
dollar see American dollar; Australian dollar; New Zealand dollar
domestic market, 21, 45, 98, 137
Drysdale, Peter, 152
DTCs see financial institutions—deposit-taking companies

economic growth, 87, 142; for New Zealand, 120
electronic funds transference, 99
employment, lifetime, 16, 67, 70
endowment insurance, 35
Eurodollar, 107
European Common Agricultural Policy, 142
European Currency Unit (ECU), 101
Euroyen bonds, 36, 39, 86, 91, 146, 147
European market see financial markets—Euroyen
exchange rates, 15, 19, 42; adjustments, 22; central bank intervention, 19, 89; floating, 53, 88, 120, 121, 127, 133; instabilities, 13, 20, 89; risk, 20, 86, 88,

93, 121, 124; *see also* Working Group
on the Yen–Dollar Exchange Rate
exports, 45, 90; *see also* trade surpluses;
from New Zealand *see* New Zealand
exports; of capital *see* capital outflow

finance, international *see* international
monetary system
financial deregulation, 20, 67, 98, 139;
and Australia, 21; and main-bank
system, 16, 25; and Pacific countries,
14, 108, 118; and personal savings,
42–3; Japanese, 15, 18, 22, 25–72, 85,
88, 105, 135; progress of, 14, 23
financial institutions, 20, 98, 133; *see also*
banks and banking; securities
companies; competition among, 37,
133; deposit-taking companies, 110;
Japanese, 14, 16, 27, 32–5, 66, 111, 114,
135; bond underwriting, 29; in Hong
Kong, 112, 115; in Singapore, 115;
ownership of, 66; lending practices, 47,
52, 60, 99, 113;
        securities, 76
financial markets, 16, 73, 87, 95, 101,
111–12; *see also* bond markets; capital
markets; futures markets; treasury
bills; Amsterdam, 102; Australia, 20,
22, 105, 135, 158; credit control and
open, 15; Euromarket, 39, 52, 102, 114;
Euroyen, 18, 19, 39, 87, 93, 107, 109,
136, 138;
        interest rates, 40
equity markets, 116; government
policies and, 21, 87, 90, 138; Hong
Kong, 20, 21, 103, 105, 110–13;
information needs, 103–4, 115;
internationalisation, 41, 50, 60, 97–9,
133, 135, 143; Japan, 18, 27–44, 60, 75,
95, 135–8;
        see also financial markets—Tokyo;
        and monetary policy, 45–54, 83;
        discount rate, 46;
        segmentation, 45, 111;
        size, 76, 85;
lenders of last resort, 20, 47, 100;
London, 98, 100, 103; Montreal, 102;
New York, 40, 100, 103;
        COMEX, 102
New Zealand, 20, 21, 105; offshore,
102, 108, 110, 150; Osaka, 117; Pacific,
14, 20–3, 97, 102–3, 105, 110; risk
avoidance, 20, 85, 99; Singapore, 20, 21,

103, 105, 110–13; Sydney, 103; Tokyo,
17, 21, 28, 85, 100–4, 147;
        offshore, 98, 102, 103, 105, 108,
        109–10, 111, 148, 150
US, 90; Vancouver, 102
Fiscal Investment and Loan Program,
Japan, 31
foreign exchange law, 1980, Japan, 15, 27
foreign exchange markets *see* financial
markets
foreign exchange rates *see* exchange rates
foreign investment: in Australia, 140; in
Japan, 113, 145; Japanese, 76, 77,
79–83, 137; by private financial
institutions, 39; by public sector, 40
foreign securities *see* securities—offshore
forex trading, 113–14
Fujii, Makoto, 10, 14, 17, 18, 20, 73, 87
fund management, 21, 116–17
futures markets, 21, 117–18; Hong Kong,
117, 118; options, 89; Singapore, 118;
Sydney, 102

gensaki market, 9, 19, 22, 40, 47, 50;
access for foreigners, 42, 144; New
Zealand use, 123
Germany, 41, 53, 58, 90
government bills, 51, 145
government bonds, 15, 19, 27, 46, 49, 103;
and Japan's fiscal deficits, 29, 48; and
small-scale investors, 35; funds, 49
government investments *see*
investment—public sector
Great Britain *see* United Kingdom
Gyōten, Toyō, 87–8

Hang Seng futures, 117
Higgins, Christopher, 10, 14, 21, 22, 105,
133, 152
Hitachi Zosen, 70
Hong Kong, 107, 108, 109, 111–13, 115;
research facilities, 116; stock market
crash, 117; tax haven, 113

India, 109, 112
Indonesia: and Japan, 78; trade surplus,
78
inflation, 19; *see also* Japan—inflation
insurance, life *see* life insurance
companies
interest rates, 48; *see also* Canadian
interest rates; United Kingdom—

interest rates; adjustment, 15, 49, 84;
and liquidity preference, 15, 137; and
savings, 43; call rate, 47; controls,
28–31, 38, 40, 42, 43; covered interest
rate parity, 40, 42; deregulation of, 14,
28, 29, 30;
   New Zealand, 120;
determination of, 14, 27, 31, 45;
non-regulated, 30; on world markets,
18, 41; risks, 20, 99; structure, 46;
uncovered interest rate parity, 41
International Banking Facility, America,
102
International Monetary Fund, 142
international monetary system, 97,
101–3, 138; competing systems, 20, 95,
98; internationalisation, 18, 21, 42, 93,
97–9; role of the yen, 11, 17, 20, 91–3,
101, 107, 138
investment: see also foreign investment
direct, 47, 79, 80; excess, 45; public
sector, 40; trust funds, 49

Japan: balance of payments, 78;
   surplus, 53;
   current account, 17;
   deficit, 45;
   surplus, 17, 43, 48, 53;
   Economic Planning Agency, 84;
   financial system, 25, 32, 45–8, 140–1;
   BOJ Net, 99;
   reform, 27, 97, 105, 144–9
   fiscal policy, 17, 48, 84; Foreign
   Exchange and Foreign Trade Control
   Law, 38, 48, 144;
   and interest rate parity, 40;
   imports, 19, 90;
   inflation, 45–6;
   investments in, 18, 31, 58–9, 136;
   labour market, 63;
   land use reform, 141;
   monetary policy, 15, 16, 28, 41, 45–54;
   and internationalisation of the yen,
   20, 89, 134; see also yen—
   internationalisation
   window guidance, 47;
   Securities and Exchange Law, 37, 46;
   trade balances, 78, 83, 84–5, 101, 136
Japan Development Bank, 51, 62
Japanese government, 18, 62
Jonson, Peter, 11

Kurushima Dockyard, 70

labour markets see Japan—labour market;
   New Zealand—labour market
Latin America, 81, 111, 137
lending rates, 46
'level playing field' concept, 98–9
life insurance companies, Japan, 13, 23,
117, 148; foreign investments, 39, 82,
145
liquidity risk, 20
loans, 15, 49–50; see also borrowing;
   interest rates; bank, 15, 46; Euroyen,
   79; excess demand, 46; long term,
   79–80; non-bank, 111; syndicated, 111

McKenzie, Colin, 10, 13, 14, 15
Maekawa, Haruo, 136, 141, 143
Malaysia: and Japan, 78; trade surplus, 78
maruyū savings system, 31, 141
mein banku sei see banks and
   banking—main-bank system
Middle East, 111; investment in Japan, 42
Minebea company, 71
Ministry of Finance, Japan, 8, 11, 27, 84;
   and deregulation, 107; and interest
   rates, 30, 152; fund raising, 113; and
   takeovers, 16, 70–1; and treasury bill
   market, 29
Ministry of International Trade and
   Industry, Japan, 8
Ministry of Ports and
   Telecommunications, Japan, 30
MITI see Ministry of International Trade
   and Industry, Japan
MOF see Ministry of Finance, Japan
monetary system, international see
   international monetary system
money see currency
money market certificates, 9, 28–9, 53,
   146; small-denomination, 30, 149
money markets see financial markets
money supply, 41, 53, 54

New Zealand, 21–2, 105, 119–32;
   borrowing, 109, 126–7;
   public sector, 22, 125–6
   current account deficit, 125; dollar, 22,
   121, 127, 128; exports, 131; imports,
   119, 131; labour market, 131; monetary
   policy, 120; Reserve Bank, 119, 120,
   122–3; tourist industry, 120; trade, 22,
   105, 119–20, 130; Treasury, 120
Nicholl, Peter, 10, 14, 19, 21, 105, 119
Nikkei futures, 117

1987 crash, 13
North America, 81; see also Canada;
    United States

Oceania, 81; see also Pacific countries
OECD see Organisation for Economic
    Cooperation and Development
oil crisis, 53, 133
Ong, Nai Pew, 10, 14, 21, 105, 107
OPEC see Organisation of Petroleum
    Exporting Countries
Organisation for Economic Cooperation
    and Development (OECD), 8, 133
Organisation of Petroleum Exporting
    Countries (OPEC), 8; funds, 102
Osaka stock exchange, 117
overseas investment see foreign
    investment

Pacific countries, 128; trade, 90
Pacific–Asian Currency Union (PACU), 8
PACU see Pacific–Asian Currency Union
pension funds, 48
Plaza Agreement, 141
postal savings system, 28, 30–1, 32, 43,
    145
primary products, 19, 78; see also
    agricultural trade
public sector borrowing see borrowing—
    public sector
public sector investments see
    investment—public sector

Rapp, W. Y., 16, 23
Reserve Bank of Australia, 22

samurai bonds, 9, 40, 94, 108, 114, 136
Saudi Arabia, 13
savings: and capital outflow, 15, 107;
    Japanese, 22, 27, 28, 85, 107, 134;
        and taxation, 42–3, 141;
        average household, 30
securities, 51, 82, 109, 152; analysis, 62,
    70; Australian, 22; government, 29, 51,
    99; see also government bills; Japanese
    facilities, 19, 29, 34, 37, 56, 99;
    Japanese holdings, 113; negotiable, 37;
    offshore, 16, 39, 82, 115, 116;
    transferable, 51; underwriting, 37; US,
    82
securities companies, 37, 40; permitted
    activities, 15, 37
shareholders, interlocking, 16
Sheard, Paul, 10, 14, 15, 16, 20, 55, 152

shibosai bonds, 9, 114
Shinkai, Yoichi, 10, 14, 17, 18, 73, 75
shipping, 90
shogun bonds, 9, 40, 108, 114, 136
short term money market, 19, 50, 52
SIMEX see Singapore International
    Monetary Exchange
Singapore, 107, 111–13, 116, 157; and
    Japan, 78, 103, 108; Central Provident
    Fund, 116
Singapore International Monetary
    Exchange (SIMEX), 8, 117
South Korea, 107, 109, 111; and Japan,
    78; trade balances, 84
Southeast Asian trade, 90–1
sterling, 94, 123, 124
Stutchbury, Michael, 10, 13
Sumitomo Bank, 66, 68–9
Suzuki, Yoshio, 10, 14, 15, 17, 19, 20, 73,
    97, 105
Swiss francs, 113, 126

Tachi, Ryuichiro, 10, 14, 15, 16, 45
Taiwan, 107, 111
Taiyo-Kobe Bank, 70
takeovers, 72; in Japan, 70; market, 20,
    25, 55, 63, 72; unfriendly, 16, 70
Tateho Chemical Company, 67, 70
taxation, 20, 42–3, 138–40; companies,
    110; reform, 43, 141; withholding tax,
    40, 110, 139
tokkin trust funds, 9, 116, 117
Tokyo offshore market, 28, 40, 41, 98,
    102, 103, 105, 108, 109–10, 111
Tokyo Stock Exchange, 8, 40, 118
tourism, 120, 130
trade negotiations, 134, 142
trade surpluses, 78, 79, 85
treasury bills, 9, 51–2; market, 16, 19, 20,
    22, 52; and Bank of Japan, 29, 52
Trust Fund Bureau, Japan, 51
TSE see Tokyo Stock Exchange

United Kingdom: and New Zealand, 120,
    130; financial dealings with, 111;
    interest rates, 41; treasury bill market,
    52
United States: bond sales to Japan, 58,
    103; capital inflow and current account
    deficits, 13; from Japan, 18, 78, 79, 80;
    current account deficit, 13, 28, 53, 101;
    dollars see American dollars; Fed wire,
    99, 157; fiscal policy, 53, 83, 84;

interest rates, 28, 41, 139; monetary
policy, 53, 84; relations with Japan, 38,
78, 152; relations with New Zealand,
130; savings rate, 43; takeover market,
63; trade balance, 17, 84; treasury bills,
51, 52, 82, 85

Venice Summit, 84, 85

Western Asian trade, 90–1
Western Europe, 110, 111
withholding tax *see* taxation—
  withholding tax
Working Group on the Yen–Dollar
  Exchange Rate, 38–9
World Bank, 85, 102, 142

world economy, 17–20, 73, 133–4, 140,
143; *see also* International monetary
system; and the yen, 87–96, 101,
123–5, 135

yen: appreciation of, 39, 78, 84; as reserve
currency, 29, 94, 138; assets *see* assets—
held in yen; in New Zealand, 21,
121–3, 126; in the Pacific, 128–32;
internationalisation of, 18, 20, 54,
87–96, 121, 129, 138; reserves, 19,
121–3
Yen–Dollar Accord of 1984, 113
Yoshitomi, M., 18, 20

zaiteku, 9, 67, 115